710,20

SKYMEN

By the same author

FLY FOR YOUR LIFE

SKYMEN

Heroes of Fifty Years of Flying

by

LARRY FORRESTER

ST. MARTIN'S PRESS   NEW YORK

For

GREGG

Library of Congress Cataloging in Publication Data

Forrester, Larry.
  Skymen: heroes of fifty years of flying.

  Reprint of the ed. published by Collins, London.
  1. Air pilots—Biography.   2. Aeronautics—History.
I. Title.
TL539.F6   1977   629.13′092′2   76-62765
ISBN 0-312-72782-8

ACKNOWLEDGMENTS

IN MY research for this book I am chiefly indebted to Mr. Peter Salton of the *Daily Express*, who with his expert knowledge, his excellent contacts and his newspaperman's eye for accuracy, dug up innumerable cuttings, checked dates, facts, figures and technical names and spellings; personally typed out a great deal of the material and, giving up an enormous amount of his spare time, helped me to accumulate a vast hoard of original matter. In a task of this kind, few authors are fortunate enough to have the enthusiastic aid of a highly-trained Fleet Street journalist.

My thanks are also due to Mr. I. C. Nerney of the Air Ministry Historical Section—and not for the first time, by any means. I owe much to the staff of the Imperial War Museum; the United States Library and Information Centre; the Science Museum, Kensington; and the Reading Room of the British Museum.

Bill Strutton, the film-writer, biographer and novelist, contributed many valuable suggestions and helped in particular with the chapter on Sir Alan Cobham. Wing Commander R. R. Stanford Tuck, D.S.O., D.F.C., gave me his permission to use material from *Fly For Your Life*, the biography of him which I wrote in 1956. For this I am also indebted to the original publishers of that work, Frederick Muller Ltd.

Some of the chapters are developed from a series of articles which I wrote for *Everybody's* some years ago under the title "Victory In the Air."

The books, British and foreign, which I have consulted

are too numerous to list here, but I wish to mention a few which not only were particularly helpful, but thoroughly enjoyable : Ralph Murche's *Song of the Sky* ; Ruth Mitchell's *My Brother Bill* ; Adolf Galland's *The First and the Last* ; Richard Hillary's superb classic *The Last Enemy* ; *While Others Sleep*, by James A. Michener and various works by that prince of air-pioneers, Alexander de Seversky. The files of various publications, such as *Flight, The Aeroplane* and *Air Facts, Time, Illustrated* and *Picture Post*, yielded a wealth of precious detail.

L. F.

AUTHOR'S PREFACE

THE SCOPE and purpose of this book require a few words of explanation. This is not a history—though it does provide an outline of aviation's development from the earliest efforts to the present day. It is a book about pilots, a collection of personal stories giving the backgrounds, characters and careers of some of the world's most famous flyers, men—and women—who have made important contributions to the conquest of the " newest element," the sky.

Now, the sky has many heroes, for in the whole story of humanity there has never been a chapter of such immense and bold activity and astounding progress as the first fifty-odd years of what may be aptly termed " the Flying Age." In that period—less than an average life-time—the frail wood, wire and cheesecloth contraption of the Wright Brothers has evolved into a thundering, whining supersonic jet-giant which has much greater horse-power than the largest locomotive and more destructive power than any battleship. And man has entered Space.

Such an achievement is the result of great endeavour by many pioneers and pilots—all men of heroic stature.

Consequently, choosing the subject for each chapter was not easy. Some illustrious names are missing, for it seemed to me pointless to try to write more about Group Captain Leonard Cheshire, V.C., after his own book *Bomber Pilot* and two excellent biographies by Russell Braddon and Andrew Boyle; or about Group Captain Douglas Bader, after Paul Brickhill's splendid *Reach for the*

7

Sky and the successful film made of it. In recent years other films have been based on the achievements of Charles Lindberg and Wing Commander Guy Gibson, V.C., leader of the " Dambusters."

So I have concentrated on those airmen, equally distinguished, whose names and adventures are not so well-known that their tales are " ancient history." To the younger reader, indeed, many of these stories should come completely fresh.

The sky is not the territory of one nation—any more than the high seas are. Its conquest has been an international affair. True, the sky often has been a bitter battleground, yet there exists between flying men of all nations a spirit of mutual respect and brotherhood which even war cannot destroy completely. Therefore I have included stories of pilots who served " on the other side "—for heroism is heroism, whatever the cause it serves, and a gallant enemy is a gallant enemy, even if his politics disgust you.

A good many of the stories, of course, have nothing to do with war. But the peace-time sky has a wealth of snares and treacheries of its own. Fighting through a raging electrical storm over jagged mountains, uninhabited jungle, or a freezing waste of ocean, with your radio jammed by static and your petrol getting low, or with ice beginning to form on your wings and your engine losing revolutions as the propeller blades get frosted—this is just as tough a battle as any involving flak and fighter formations, and it calls for just as much skill and cool-headed courage.

So does the lonely, life-time battle fought by the far-seeing, dedicated pioneer against official obstruction or indifference—men like Britain's Frank Whittle and America's Billy Mitchell, who risked their careers, and ruined their health by years of overwork and endless setbacks, because each believed what he was doing was right for the future of his country, and for the future of flying. And so does the deliberate gamble of the top test pilot when he takes up a new, experimental machine and puts it into a screaming dive; and the devotion of the flight surgeon who, doing research on the physical effects of supersonic flying, submits his body to extreme pressures and tremendous velocities; and the great-hearted gallantry of pioneer astronauts like Russia's Yuri Gagarin, and Alan Shepard of the U.S. Navy, riding rockets into the weightless void, beginning the quest of the cosmos; and the humaneness of the Swiss rescue pilot who braves blizzards and lands his frail machine on icy, sloping shelves of the upper Alps to reach injured climbers or skiers—no, it doesn't take a war to produce flying heroes!

So much for the scope of this book—its purpose in the main is to provide some idea of the very special qualities which, in the world of flying, produce individuals of outstanding skill and bravery. These qualities are very hard to define, for they vary from case to case according to social background, nationality and the particular field of achievement, and of course a certain amount of luck is required to provide the opportunity for special talent to be demonstrated. But a basic essential of greatness, present in all flying heroes, seems to be a fierce pride in their work.

Again and again, in examining the careers of great airmen I have found this common driving force—pride making the young pilot practise long and hard, and practice bringing him close to perfection, making him so well-drilled that when danger develops he corrects or counters *automatically*, memory operating his reflexes and guiding his hands and feet. . . . Pride making him get to know his machine— every rivet and rib, every tiny weakness and each last limit of its reliability—until it has become like a part of him, like an extension of his own limbs and body, sensitive to the slightest whim of his mind or tremor of his instinct. . . . Pride making him establish the closest possible understanding with his mechanics, and the men with whom he flies. . . . And when at last the testing time comes, in the instant of high peril, it is pride that feeds him courage, that holds him to his purpose—because this is what he has been working for, rehearsing for, so long and so thoroughly, and to turn back now would be a wasteful and shameful action. . . .

One thing is certain—heroes often may be casual, but they are never careless. Only a very careless flyer, a man with no real pride in his workmanship, could utter any of the following phrases—which Royal Air Force men give as classic examples of " famous last words " :

"*It's over in that direction somewhere.*"

"*Don't worry—I know these mountains like the back of my hand.*"

"*Fuel? We've plenty—that gauge always under-reads.*"

"*Flight plan? Forget it, chum—I could navigate this trip with my eyes shut.*"

"*What did the Met boys say about thunderheads?*"

"*There's old Archie taking off—let's nip down and give him a scare!*"

"*Control's bearing must be wrong—I just know we couldn't be that far off course.*"

"*Where did I put my oxygen mask?*"

"*Why should I check the magnetos? That's the ground chief's job.*"

"*There's where my girl lives—let's drop in!*"

"*I'm not turning back just because of a little rudder vibration.*"

Men who talk like that don't live long enough to earn distinction! Can you imagine any of these words coming from the lips of great airmen such as Alan Cobham, Stanford Tuck or John Derry? No, such men are too sensible, too thorough. Too proud.

In addition to this strong, personal pride, the earnest young airman of to-day draws strength from " tradition " —which is simply another sort of pride: the collective pride which a nation, a squadron or a civil company takes in the achievements of its predecessors, together with the resolve to do as well, or even better. The victories, sacrifices and patient pioneerings of the past are a constant, if sometimes sub-conscious, example to the serious-minded newcomer.

Thus pride—personal and traditional—sets a high standard in so many things, and ever strives to raise those standards still higher. It can be thought of as a process— a constant sifting, a selecting of the best material—all the time preparing *potential* leaders and heroes. Fate, of course, makes the final selection, by providing the circumstances in which some of those potential leaders and heroes can become *actual*.

Now, precisely what constitutes " the best material "? Obviously certain natural aptitudes (e.g. a mind which can grasp technicalities; quick reflexes, and the ability to co-ordinate physical actions) and a certain standard of general intelligence are necessary, but beyond that it is difficult to formulate rules. For in appearance, background and personality, air heroes do not seem to follow any set pattern. Some are boisterous, full of nervous energy; some are withdrawn, bookish men. . . . Others are out-wardly reckless—mischievous almost; one or two seem fussy, over-cautious. . . . Yet others appear to be remarkably casual, laconic, uninspired ; a few are frankly, joyously eccentric. They represent a strange cross-section of international society—from English public school boy to American Indian ranch-hand, from Italian merchant's son to Russian peasant, from Prussian aristocrat to Edinburgh bank-teller. And this haphazard mixture is greatly increased in war-time, when air forces expand vastly and outstanding pilots develop who, but for the national call, would have remained quietly at office desk, factory bench or University, and in all probability never entered the cockpit of an aircraft.

On one R.A.F. squadron I flew with during World War Two, there were three very successful, highly decorated pilots ; one was the son of a Welsh miner, another the heir to an English Earldom, and the third a West Indian lad whose grandparents had been slaves on a Barbados plantation.

So, it seems to me a fair conclusion that national characteristics, social status and individual personality have nothing to do with the making of an air hero. The sky has no racial or class distinctions, and it is not " type "-conscious ; it is a highly democratic world in which only ability counts, where skill and experience earn swift advancement and, for those special few, glory.

A good many of the young people who read this book are going to make their careers in, or closely connected with, the steadily growing aircraft industries and the great, globe-spanning commercial air-lines. Though ballistic missiles are changing the role of the air forces, pilots, navigators and ground crews are still needed, and always will be—so others will join the services. Some, no doubt, will help to design, build and operate cosmic-ships probing for other planets—and a few will fly these ships. I hope this book will provide them with a compact record of what has gone before, and with some knowledge of those who have made important contributions to the building of civil and military air-power. I hope, too, that it may dispel from their minds the old fallacious notion that heroes are some kind of supermen—that " heroes are born, not made." In short, that heroes are some sort of privileged class, or " closed shop," and that outsiders, no matter how enthusiastic, hard-working and naturally gifted, can never be admitted. This is wicked nonsense.

Let young people take courage from the factual evidence. First, let them get it quite straight that a hero is not a man without fear, but one whose special qualities—particularly the aforementioned " pride in work "—enable him to cope with it, to control it, to prevent it from impairing his judgment or interfering with his actions. Second, let them see that a hero is not necessarily endowed with great bodily strength—Micky Mannock had defective vision, Wiley Post was one-eyed, Billy Mitchell had a serious heart complaint, and Frank Whittle was twice rejected by R.A.F. medical boards (to say nothing of the legendary " Tin Legs " Bader, limbless fighter ace !)

True, no man sets out deliberately to become a hero— ambition alone is never enough, and in fact denotes a self-interest which is liable to destroy the sense of duty and the team-spirit which, nine times out of ten, are essential to success. Yet any man with the right aptitudes, who takes sincere pride in his job, who never ceases to learn and to practise, to try to improve, need not impose a limit on himself in aviation—it is perfectly possible that, given the opportunity, he may display heroic mettle.

In other words, my view is that in flying no one becomes a hero by design, nor yet by accident—but by a little of each and, most important, by a great deal of honest labour !

Another purpose of this book is to remind this generation that the first men into Space travelled by courtesy of Orville and Wilbur Wright, Amelia Earhart, John Paul Stapp and the others.

In 1903, before this half-century of astounding progress —" the Flying Age "—began, most people were saying man would never get into the air ; now, with the outstanding success of both Russian and American astronauts, no one doubts for a moment that momentous events lie ahead, close ahead; that flights to other worlds, for instance, must become reality in the very next stage of development.

For in aviation, more clearly than in any other field of human endeavour, it has been demonstrated that man is subject to no restrictions other than those imposed by his own imagination, technical skill and courage.

Larry Forrester.

SKYMEN

This Book's Roll of Honour:

ORVILLE and WILBUR WRIGHT (*U.S.A.*) Gold Medal (French Academy of Sciences); Chevalier, Legion of Honour.

SIR GEORGE CAYLEY (*Britain*) Baronet.

OTTO LILIENTHAL (*Germany*).

JOSEPH and JACQUES MONTGOLFIER (*France*).

JEAN FRANÇOIS PILÂTRE DE ROZIER (*France*).

ALBERTO SANTOS-DUMONT (*Brazil*) Grand Officer, Legion of Honour.

LOUIS BLÉRIOT (*France*) Chevalier, Legion of Honour.

HENRI FARMAN (*Britain and France*) Chevalier, Legion of Honour.

AIR COMMODORE C. R. SAMSON (*Britain*) D.S.O., and bar; A.F.C.; Croix de Guerre (with palm); Chevalier, Legion of Honour.

COMMANDER F. H. DUNNING, R.N. (*Britain*).

BARON MANFRED VON RICHTHOFEN (*Germany*) Iron Cross (1st. Class and 2nd. Class); Medal of Merit; Military Service Cross (Austria).

CAPTAIN ROY BROWN (*Canada*) D.S.O.; D.S.C., and bar.

CAPTAIN ALBERT BALL (*Britain*) V.C.; D.S.O., and two bars; M.C.; Legion of Honour; Order of St. George (Russia).

MAJOR JAMES BYFORD MCCUDDEN (*Britain*) V.C.; D.S.O., and bar; M.C., and bar; M.M.; Croix de Guerre.

RENÉ FONCK (*France*) Croix d'Officier, Legion of Honour (28 palms); M.C. (Gt. Britain); Croix de Guerre (Belgium).

MAJOR EDWARD MANNOCK (*Britain*) V.C.; D.S.O., and two bars; M.C., and bar.

CHARLES NUNGESSER (*France*) D.S.C. (U.S.); M.C. (Gt. Britain); Croix de Guerre (France); Croix de Guerre (Belgium).

AIR MARSHAL W. A. BISHOP (*Canada*) V.C.; D.S.O.; M.C.; Croix de Chevalier, Legion of Honour; D.F.C.; Croix de Guerre (with palm).

SIR ALAN COBHAM (*Britain*) Gold Medal (Royal Aero Club); Senior Medal, Royal I.A.E.; Aviation Medal (Inst. of Transport).

BRIGADIER-GENERAL W. MITCHELL (*U.S.A.*) D.S.C.; D.S.M. (U.S.); Croix de Guerre (5 palms); Commander Legion of Honour; Companion St. Michael and St. George (Gt. Britain); Medal for Merit in War and Grand Crown Officer of Italy.

ALEXANDER DE SEVERSKY (*U.S.A.*) U.S. Medal for Merit; Knight of St. George; Officer, Legion of Honour.

COLONEL JAMES DOOLITTLE (*U.S.A.*) Congressional Medal of Honour; D.S.M., and oak leaf cluster; Silver Star; D.F.C., and two oak leaves; Bronze Star; Air Medal; Knight Commander of the Bath (Gt. Britain).

AMELIA EARHART (*U.S.A.*) D.F.C. (U.S.); Chevalier, Legion of Honour; Gold Medal (Nat. Geog. Socy.).

FRANK HAWKS (*U.S.A.*) Harman Trophy; French Aero Club Medal.

AIR MARSHAL ITALO BALBO (*Italy*) Knight Grand Cross, S. Maurizio and S. Lazzaro; Air Force Gold Medal for Military Valour; Commander, Order of the Crown of Italy; Commander, Order of the Star of Italy.

WILEY POST (*U.S.A.*).

WILL ROGERS (*U.S.A.*).

HAROLD GATTY (*U.S.A.*).

AIR VICE-MARSHAL W. E. STATON (*Britain*) C.B.E.; D.S.O., and bar; M.C.; D.F.C., and bar.

WING COMMANDER R. R. STANFORD TUCK (*Britain*) D.S.O.; D.F.C., and two bars.

FLYING OFFICER J. KAIN (*New Zealand*) D.F.C.

GROUP CAPTAIN DOUGLAS BADER (*Britain*) D.S.O., and bar; D.F.C., and bar; Legion of Honour; Croix de Guerre.

GROUP CAPTAIN A. G. MALAN (*South Africa*) D.S.O.; D.F.C., and bar.

FLIGHT LIEUTENANT JOHN CRUICKSHANK (*Britain*) V.C.

FLIGHT SERGEANT J. GARNETT (*Britain*) D.F.M.

AIR COMMODORE SIR CHARLES KINGSFORD SMITH (*Australia*) K.B.E.; M.C.

C. P. T. ULM (*Australia*).

WING COMMANDER GUY GIBSON (*Britain*) V.C.; D.S.O.; D.F.C.

WING COMMANDER " MICKY " MARTIN (*Australia*) D.S.O.; D.F.C., and two bars.

FLIGHT LIEUTENANT ROBERT HAY (*Australia*) D.F.C., and bar.

SQUADRON LEADER DAVID SHANNON (*Australia*) D.S.O., and bar; D.F.C., and bar.

PILOT OFFICER RAWDON HUME MIDDLETON (*Australia*) V.C.

FLIGHT LIEUTENANT LESLIE KNIGHT (*Australia*) D.S.O.

SQUADRON LEADER JACK LEGGO (*Australia*) D.F.C., and bar.

FLYING OFFICER " SPAM " SPAFFORD (*Australia*) D.F.C.; D.F.M.

SQUADRON LEADER C. W. PEARCE (*Australia*) D.F.C.

GROUP CAPTAIN HUGH IDWAL EDWARDS (*Australia*) V.C.

RICHARD PEARSE (*New Zealand*).

JEAN BATTEN (*New Zealand*).

SERGEANT PILOT J. A. WARD (*New Zealand*) V.C.

WING COMMANDER ALAN DEERE (*New Zealand*) D.S.O.; O.B.E.; D.F.C., and bar; D.F.C. (U.S.); Croix de Guerre with Plume.

CAPTAIN HANNA REITSCH (*Germany*) Iron Cross (1st. Class and 2nd. Class); Military Flying Medal; Gold Medal for Military Flying (with Brilliants).

AMY JOHNSON (*Britain*) C.B.E.

COLONEL MARINA RASKOVA (*U.S.S.R.*) Order of Lenin.

LIEUTENANT-COLONEL N. KEZARINOVE (*U.S.S.R.*) Order of Lenin; Red Star.

CAPTAIN A. TIMOFEYEVA (*U.S.S.R.*) Order of Lenin.

SQUADRON LEADER JOHN DERRY (*Britain*) D.F.C.; B.L. (Netherlands); Gold Medal (Royal Aero Club).

GROUP CAPTAIN FRANK WHITTLE (*Britain*) C.B.E.

CAPTAIN GEOFFREY DE HAVILLAND (*Britain*) C.B.E.; A.F.C.; D.F.C., and bar; R.D.I.

SQUADRON LEADER NEVILLE DUKE (*Britain*) D.S.O.; D.F.C.

HERMANN GEIGER (*Switzerland*).

CAPTAIN JACK SLADE (*Australia*).

THE VERY REVEREND JOHN FLYNN (*Australia*).

SQUADRON LEADER H. G. HEZELDEN (*Britain*) D.F.C., and bar.

FLIGHT LIEUTENANT D. BROOMFIELD (*Britain*) D.F.M.

FLIGHT LIEUTENANT R. ECCLESTONE (*Britain*) D.F.C.

COLONEL JOHN PAUL STAPP (*U.S.A.*). Legion of Merit (with oak leaf cluster); Cheney Award (U.S.A.F.); John Jeffries Award for Medical Research; Air Power Award for Science.

CONTENTS

ILLUSTRATIONS

CHAPTER ONE

WOOD, WIRE AND CHEESECLOTH

THE HURRICANE sliced in from the leaden Atlantic and struck North Carolina's Outer Banks at a desolate place known as Kitty Hawk. The little camp amid the barren dunes was ripped apart.

When the fury had passed, Wilbur and Orville Wright came out of the wreckage of their lean-to storehouse and silently, wearily, began to pick up the pieces. Their " flying machine "—a clumsy, kite-like construction of wood and cheesecloth, forty feet across the wings, with an automobile engine, naked and seemingly precariously balanced in the middle of it—was seriously damaged, and it would take weeks to repair it.

But the Wright Brothers, bicycle mechanics from Dayton, Ohio, were well-used to cruel setbacks like this. For four years now they had come to camp on this remote expanse of sand and experiment with their machine, and they had yet to get it an inch off the ground. This wasn't the first time a howling " twister " had ripped along the dunes, scattering their light and laboriously fashioned equipment, dashing sections of it to fragments, carrying others far out to sea. And each time they made their repairs, and got back to their experiments, they were faced with fresh disappointments ; one idea after another had to be scrapped, their theories modified, more money spent. . . .

At the week-ends trippers came out to stare at the " cranks " and make cumbrous jokes about the machine

—for hadn't Simon Newcomb, the famous American physicist, stated that it was definitely impossible to fly a heavier-than-air device? To the average person, in 1903, the idea of taking to the air in a machine which had no gas-balloon attached was no less ridiculous than the idea of a man going for a walk under the ocean without any sort of diving gear. But the two slim, dark, serious-faced young men kept their heads down over their work and ignored the braying laughter; when they lifted their tired eyes, it was to squint apprehensively at a sky once more darkening and filling with the whip and whine of a nor'-easter.

Looking back now, over more than half a century, it is hard to see where these quiet, unknown and apparently unqualified Americans, so alone, and so at odds with the views of their country's most distinguished scientists and engineers, found the strength to keep going in the face of such cruel and constant discouragement. Certainly history offered them little inspiration—from the dawn of time, the story of Man's efforts to claw his way up from the surface of the planet was little more than a mixture of fable and fiasco.

In Greek mythology, Daedalus and his son Icarus had fashioned wings of feathers, but their flight over the Mediterranean ended in tragedy when the sun's heat melted the bee's wax with which the wings were attached to their bodies. . . . Arab tales of " magic carpets " were as old and numerous as the desert's grains of sand. . . .

The incredibly versatile mind of Italy's Renaissance genius Leonardo da Vinci had conceived a design for a flying machine which was aerodynamically sound, but his age could provide neither the proper materials to build it, nor the source of power to drive it, and so it remained a useless, forgotten scrap of paper. . . .

Over the centuries in every land, various maniacs, " magicians " and misguided inventors had been hurling themselves to destruction from towers and clifftops, wildly flapping wings of feathers, sail-cloth or wood. More than once, church and state had declared such attempts sacrilegious—Man was not meant to draw nearer Heaven, except in spirit. . . . Hundreds of years of failure and official condemnation resulted in " bird-men " and builders of " sky ships " becoming as discredited as the horde of alchemists who, wandering from court to court, long-bearded and mystical, since pre-Christian times had been claiming the ability to transmute base metals into purest gold by a process known as " the secret of the Philosopher's Stone "—but never once proved it. . . .

And yet there were *some* stories worthy of serious study. There was conclusive evidence that as early as 1852 a wealthy and somewhat eccentric Englishman, Sir George Cayley, had constructed at his Yorkshire home, Brompton Hall, a crude sort of man-carrying glider which had made at least one successful flight. But Cayley, being corpulent, elderly and perhaps a little uncertain, was said to have refused to test the contrivance himself, and a reluctant, terrified coachman was forced to take the controls. (If the story is true, then this humble serving man, of whom we know almost nothing—not even his name!—was the world's first true air pilot. Directly after landing, pallid and perspiring, he gave notice, explaining in broad Yorkshire : " Ah coom t'drive coach, not t'fly like blessed bird.") At any rate, for one reason or another, Cayley's activities brought him such derision and enmity from his neighbours that he abandoned his experiments, leaving no worthwhile testimonial record. Only letters and diaries kept by his sister and other members of the family survived to prove beyond doubt that the amateur scientist had in fact overcome the basic problems of heavier-than-air flight.

At the end of the nineteenth century, a German engineer whose hobby was ornithology (the study of birds), had made flights of up to twenty seconds in home-made gliders. His name was Otto Lilienthal. On 9th August, 1896, he crashed and died, but he left valuable records of his work and a number of brilliantly written scientific papers.

Despite the countless follies and catastrophes of past ages, and the pitifully few genuine advances, the Wright Brothers remained infected by a fiery faith in the impossible, and Lilienthal was their hero. They were convinced that now they had something that none of their predecessors had possessed, a source of power compact and light enough to drive their machine through the air—the internal combustion engine. This comparatively recent invention, so successfully demonstrated in the rapidly developing "horseless carriage," or motor-car, seemed to them the key to the main problem which had defeated all the previous, serious air-pioneers. And they knew that other men, in France and other countries, thought the same and were working on experiments similar to their own.

Perhaps, too, they drew comfort from the knowledge that the only previous human invasion of the sky had resulted from the discovery of two brothers. On 5th June, 1783, Joseph and Jacques Montgolfier, of Annonay, France, had sent the world's first balloon soaring one-and-a-half miles across country in ten minutes. The following September, before the King and Queen of France at Versailles, a Montgolfier balloon rose to 1,500 feet, and stayed aloft for eight minutes, travelling about two miles, with three passengers—a sheep, a cock and a duck. The first officially recognised aerial travellers, suspended in a cage beneath the giant bag—105 feet in circumference—were unharmed by the experience. A month later a courageous court official, Jean François Pilâtre de Rozier, made the first of many successful ascents—and " the great Balloon Age " began, with daring " flights " being made regularly throughout Europe before vast and excited crowds.

But balloons did not truly fly—filled with gas which made them lighter than air, they rose into the upper, thinner atmosphere and then floated, drifted, like wood on water, at the mercy of wind and current. All manner of weird steering and " driving " devices had been tried, including huge oars protruding from the sides, with which the occupant was supposed to row his way across the sky ; but it had become very clear that the balloonist could never have more than extremely limited control over his craft.

The Montgolfier Brothers had shown merely that it was possible for Man to enter the sky without harm or discomfort : now the Wright Brothers, a hundred and twenty years later, were resolved to show that the sky could be navigated, ranged at will, in time—conquered.

On 17th December, 1903, at Kill Devil Hill, Kitty Hawk, the flimsy framework of wood, wire and cheesecloth which the inventors called an " aero-plane " was repaired once more. Jerkily, it started forward across the hard-packed sands. It had no wheels. The undercarriage consisted of a low truck which ran on sixty feet of rail laid along the beach. Driven by two propellers, the machine weighed 605 pounds, including the very noisy engine.

Gathering speed, rocking and vibrating, it roared along its rail, Wilbur Wright manipulating the makeshift controls, Orville running along after him, clothes flapping in the slipstream, his face a desperate mixture of eagerness and anxiety. Five islanders, members of the local Lifesaving Service, stood well back by the dunes, watching uneasily —the only people in this part of North Carolina who had responded to an open invitation from the brothers to come and see them " fly."

And as they watched, expecting only disaster, the noise of the machine suddenly changed, became smoother. The launching truck was slowing, falling behind, and there was daylight—empty air—between the machine and the ground. . . .

Rocking a little, rising and dipping gently, only a few feet above the sand, the contraption continued along the beach for more than five hundred feet before it flopped down lightly and slid to a stop on its landing skids. The Wrights, glowing with restrained excitement, measured and noted the distance covered and the time taken, carefully inspected their plane, then brought it back to the starting place and prepared for another attempt.

Four times that day, before the tiny group of marvelling island folk, the Wright Brothers got their craft into the air, and kept it there, moving forward in controlled flight, the last time for as long as 59 seconds, covering 852 feet.

Many years were to pass before the importance of this achievement and the heroic efforts of the brothers gained recognition in their own country. At first, most American scientists and newspaper editors simply refused to believe the accounts of those who had witnessed " aeroplane flights "—even though in 1905 Wilbur Wright, in an improved machine, covered 24 miles in 39 minutes !

What now must be rated as one of the most significant events of the twentieth century, at the time caused hardly a ripple of attention within the United States. But three thousand miles away, in France, the birth of the aeroplane on that lonely, wind-battered stretch of Carolina coast caused great excitement, and no little consternation—for various groups of scientists and engineers, working on a bewildering variety of theories and projects, had hoped to claim the honour for their own country.

Prominent among these pioneers in France was Alberto Santos-Dumont, a wealthy Brazilian. In 1898, he had built and flown a cylindrical balloon with a petrol engine. In 1901, he produced a crude form of airship which won a prize, and engendered hysterical excitement in Paris, by making the first flight from St. Cloud around the Eiffel Tower and back. Two years later, at Neuilly, he constructed the world's first airship station, where he soon built up a vast and varied collection of dirigibles.

Now, inspired by the Wright Brothers' flight, he turned his attention to designing aeroplanes, modelled on their machine. In August of 1906, he got his "No. 14 *bis*" biplane into the air for eight seconds, and in November covered 720 feet in 21 and one-fifth seconds. Immense crowds at Bagatelle acclaimed him as a public hero.

Unlike the Americans, the volatile French—conditioned, perhaps, by the thrills of "the great Balloon Age"—looked upon this new form of flying as first class public entertainment, and made a craze of it. And, unlike the quiet, absorbed Wright Brothers, Santos-Dumont did not hesitate to "play to the gallery"—to encourage ordinary people to take an interest in aeroplanes by every possible stunt and trick of showmanship.

In a matter of a few months, aero clubs were being formed thoughout the country. New periodicals appeared, specialising in "aeronautical news and adventure stories." In backyards and barns from one end of France to the other young enthusiasts hammered and sawed and tinkered, creating their contraptions—and with remarkable daring, and a good deal of luck, one by one they got into the air. These backyard builders included many who were to become famous names in aviation—Henri Farman (who later designed and manufactured the famous Farman biplane) ; master-pilot Delagrange, and the amazing, versatile Jean Louis Blériot.

Blériot was chubby, cheerful, incredibly energetic, with a large " walrus " moustache that seemed to flutter when he laughed or got excited. By 1908, he had workshops at Neuilly and a shed at Issy, and had survived nearly fifty crashes. That was the year that Wilbur Wright, despairing of his own government's attitude and fearing that Europe would steal the lead in aviation development, got the idea of taking the latest Wright machine to France and entering the various flying competitions and displays which by now were regular events there.

Many French enthusiasts resented the American's " intrusion," but Louis Bleriot organised a welcoming committee. And when it was found that Wright's machine had been damaged in the Trans-Atlantic voyage, Louis rushed to offer him the facilities of his Neuilly workshops, and any personal help needed to make the repairs.

Wright's French tour began in July, with a demonstration at Le Mans—now a famous motor-racing track, scene of the annual 24-hour Grand Prix d'Endurance event. He gave what must have been the world's first display of a new art, " aerobatics." Banked almost vertically, he turned repeatedly in a circle of just under 31 yards diameter, close above the upturned faces of a huge and wildly demonstrative crowd, then described perfect figure-eights, suddenly swooped down to the gentlest of landings, with his wings reaching the horizontal at the same instant as he touched the ground.

Blériot ran to congratulate him, declared again and again : " This Wright machine is definitely superior to any of ours."

Soon after this, Louis scrapped several of his planes and, in a frantic burst of work, designed and produced a 28-horsepower aircraft with a light framework, only part of which was covered with fabric. This, his eleventh plane, cruised at 40 m.p.h., and after testing her—with unusual secrecy—he expressed the highest satisfaction.

On 25th July, 1909, in this primitive craft—with his burly body jammed into the tiny cockpit, and his big moustache fluttering in the wind—Jean Louis Blériot crossed the English Channel from Calais to the Dover cliffs. He covered the 25 miles in 37 minutes, despite violent air currents over the water. And he did it " by following my nose "—without a compass.

Not just France, or England, but the entire civilised world at last awoke to the serious potentialities of this new device, the aeroplane. Blériot's feat was infinitely more impressive than anything that had been done before, because it had a great underlying significance that was clear to all nations. For the first time a flying machine had travelled from one country to another, across an expanse of open sea which throughout past ages had been a comforting barrier, a shield. . . .

Thus Louis Blériot, the cheerful backyard tinkerer, became an international hero whose achievement transformed, almost overnight, military and social thinking about national boundaries. From the moment that he thumped down, awkwardly and gratefully, on the clifftops at Dover, the world seemed to shrink, and nations felt closer to, and more aware of, each other.

Louis went on to many more successes. In 1912, he became the first man to "loop the loop," and before his death in 1936, he designed more than 300 types of aircraft, including several successful war machines, and built over 10,000 planes. Few men have made greater single contributions to aviation.

Like the Wright Brothers, he was one of the architects of a new and astounding age. An age of incredibly rapid development in which men of all nations, rising after the pioneer brothers of Kitty Hawk, lifted humanity to an enlargement of life which our forefathers—and perhaps the Wright Brothers themselves—would never have dreamed possible.

CHAPTER TWO

STRONG MEN AND STOUT SHIPS

IT WAS 1911. The Kaiser was already strutting across Europe with boasts of his formidable army. Germany's neighbours grew more and more fearful, aware that he was building up the finest fighting machine in the world.

But the Kaiser and his Prussian warlords knew they were still far from supreme—they had an " Achilles' heel." The British navy—whether patrolling distant shores of the Empire, paying courtesy visits to foreign ports, or merely riding at anchor in the summer waters of the Mediterranean —was a constant reminder that whatever power the German army could bring to bear on Europe, any war against Great Britain in the end must be won on the high seas. With this in mind, the Kaiser laid the first keels of what were to become the ships of the Grand Fleet.

Yet while the Kaiser was parading his soldiers and brooding over sea-power, the English seemed to be interested only in keeping open their great trade links from the Port of London. So it was that the Royal Navy—for over a hundred years the traditional rulers of the world's seas —had little time to explore and exploit new methods of attack and defence ; without any serious rival, there appeared to be little need. . . .

There were a few individuals, of course, whose thirst for adventure and natural curiosity forced them, even against the temper of the times, to think of the business of

war. Such a man was Charles Rumney Samson, a dapper
naval lieutenant with a Satanic red beard, a vile temper—
and an uncanny inventive talent. This son of a Manchester
solicitor had become a midshipman in 1899, and served
in the Pomone campaign of 1903. But his story does not
really start until eight years later, when the Royal Navy
was loaned planes and an aerodrome so that a few officers
could be taught to fly.

Volunteers were called for ; in the first rush two hundred
submitted their names. Samson was one of the four
accepted. In October of the same year, he completed his
flying course with distinction, and became the first commanding officer of the Royal Navy station at Eastchurch,
Isle of Sheppey.

That appointment led to many a headache for the
traditionalists of the Admiralty. Not many days had passed
before this sprightly little man was badgering his senior
officers to buy two new-type training planes, and to send
him naval ratings to form the nucleus of a naval flying
school. The Admiralty, long experienced in disciplining
the enthusiastic unorthodoxy of juniors, could not shake
off Samson. Like his Old Testament namesake, the man
burned with faith and possessed a strength that would not
be denied. The Admiralty capitulated by the end of the
year, and Samson jocularly considered the two planes they
sent him as " a Christmas gift from their Lordships."

Within the next month he was back pestering Whitehall
with an even more outrageous request : now he wanted
to convert a ship of the line, the doughty H.M.S. *Africa*,
into a " platform " from which he could fly an aeroplane !

The first answer from his superiors was summed up in
one word—" ridiculous." A certain highly placed naval
man went so far as to say : " Samson, rather than being

like a gentleman of His Majesty's navy, is more suited to be a circus clown ! "

Such rebuffs only made Samson bad-tempered and more persistent. There were times in this " battle for a floating platform " when he even hectored and argued with admirals, completely disregarding the fact that at one stroke these men could end his career. They were staggered, stunned by the concentration of effort, the variety of approaches and procedures, the persistence—in turn patronising, threatening, and downright abusive—which this extraordinary man was able to deploy in order to get what he wanted.

Samson's strength won the day : on a cold January morning in 1912 he flew one of his little training planes from Eastchurch to Sheerness. With all the hostile fussiness of an old maid watching a stranger fondle her cat, he supervised the machine's loading aboard *Africa*. Then carefully, with his own naval ratings, he manoeuvred the plane into the best position for a take-off from the warship's short deck.

When all was ready Samson paused, looked round him, surveying the faces of the watching ship's officers and men. In all their eyes he could read the same thought—" this poor idiot, for no apparent reason wants to launch his rickety flying machine, this awkward-looking structure of struts and wires and canvas, from this short and gently pitching deck, and in just a few minutes he is going to be dead or, at best, gravely injured. . . ." Infuriated by their expressions, Samson climbed into his cockpit glowering and muttering, in a foul temper, shouted his last, peremptory orders. The ratings fussed round the machine, the engine fired, and then the plane started to roll forward— slowly, much too slowly it seemed.

Up on the bridge the captain of the *Africa* moved his lips in silent blasphemies, braced himself for the disaster he considered inevitable. He had consented to this madcap experiment only under continued pressure. He had no use for aeroplanes—smelly, undignified, unreliable contraptions, a passing fad—and if this young stunt-man wanted to commit suicide he'd sooner he did so elsewhere, and didn't make a nasty mess on *his* shining decks. . . .

The plane lurched on towards the bows, not gaining much speed, seeming to waddle like some clumsy duck. Then, to everyone's great surprise, quite suddenly it lifted into the air. Samson had got his craft airborne, all right— but now it seemed that it just hung there, a few feet above the boards, engine revving madly, wings waggling slightly, struts and wires blurred in violent vibration. The little engine clanking full blast, the flimsy plane could make no progress—it was all it could do to keep up with the steaming warship! Then all at once, just for a few seconds the fairly strong headwind fell away: slowly, yet steadily enough, Samson climbed, cleared the *Africa's* forward rigging and drew ahead. The officers and men who had watched him with pitying eyes only a few minutes before now cheered wildly and waved their arms as the tiny plane soared higher, then came round to circle the ship in salute.

Senior naval men who witnessed this flight agreed that Samson had great skill and courage, but they still could not see the point of his demonstration. It was one thing to get an aircraft off from a warship's deck—but to land it again obviously was impossible. Supposing in time of war, somewhere on the wide ocean a pilot took off, flew ahead of the fleet and spotted enemy units—how could he get his information to the commander? Dropping messages in special containers on a relatively small, fast-moving target was at best a chancy business—and in those days, of course, no wireless communication was possible between an aircraft and land or sea stations. Nor were parachutes invented—what was to become of the pilot if he was out of range of land? Were these proposed " aerial spotters " to be a suicide force? And what about the immense cost in lost machines?

Moreover, Samson's success at the first attempt was no guarantee that planes could take off regularly from dread-noughts, or that other pilots would prove as capable. And, of course, weather conditions would have to be almost perfect for them even to try. . . .

When he heard of these reactions, Samson exploded into a characteristic rage. Did they take him for a wild, glory-seeking gambler, a mere acrobat, a vain and empty-headed death-defier? Hadn't he submitted comprehensive reports of his researches and theories? Didn't they realise that what was needed, what he was campaigning for, *was a new type of naval vessel, specially designed to carry aircraft, on which planes not only could take-off but also land again?*

For many weeks, on a specially marked-out section of the airfield he had practised take-offs and landings in every sort of weather that was " flyable " by the standards of the time. (It must be remembered that the world's first powered flight, by the Wright Brothers, had been made only about nine years before!) Using special techniques, he had found he could get airborne and set the plane down in a sur-prisingly short distance, and from these results he cal-culated the minimum safety length of run needed on board a steaming ship. This was appreciably less than on the land, for the vessel's forward speed was a " bonus " which could be deducted from the normal take-off speed of the aircraft. In other words, if an aircraft on land normally

took off at 50 miles an hour, then from a ship moving at
ten miles an hour it would rise from the deck at an indicated
speed of 40. Of course allowance had to be made for wind
—a ten mile an hour wind blowing from the stern would
cancel out the " bonus." But it was a simple matter for the
ship to turn into wind—and then the wind speed provided
an additional aid, and the length of take-off run was even
shorter.

And everything that applied to the take-off held good for
landing, provided the pilots were specially trained. Perhaps in time, he had suggested, not only the ships but the
planes themselves could be specially designed for this
work.

The very next day, still incensed and determined to prove
he was working on a sound scientific basis, Samson flew
his machine from the deck of H.M.S. *Hibernia*, an even
shorter run. The ship was steaming at ten-and-a-half
knots into a light breeze; he submitted figures which
showed that on land it would have been impossible to
get airborne in such a short distance. This time several
technically-minded experts at the Admiralty sat up with a
jerk, discussed Samson's report at length, planned a
programme of research and development which, many
years later, was to give the Navy wings. Samson, single-
handed and in the face of stern opposition and no little
scorn, had laid the foundations of the Royal Naval Air
Service.

But typically, as soon as he was satisfied that Admiralty
had taken note of his ideas, and at last apparently intended
to do something about them, he switched his attention to
other problems. By the summer of that year he had submitted valuable reports on the trajectory of aerial bombs,
and suggestions for aiming and fusing. The following

year—1913—he began a project that seemed to his fellow officers, and even his most ardent admirers, infinitely crazier, and more pointless, than the business of flying off from a ship.

He actually started trying to fly at night! In complete darkness, he piloted his plane round and round Eastchurch. And by the sparse light of a few oil flares laid out on the airfield, somehow he even contrived to make very respectable landings.

By now their Lordships of the Admiralty were beginning to recognise that this ill-tempered " circus clown " was leading the world in new aviation techniques. They ordered full investigation of his proposals for night-flying instruments and airfield lighting. He was promoted Commander. And at the Review of the Fleet at Spithead in July 1914 he introduced yet another technique—leading two flights of three planes each in a V-formation. This was the first time that such a formation had been used—except by wild geese !

When war broke out a few months later he was posted to Skegness as commander of a detachment of planes patrolling the East Coast. But later he took his squadron to Ostend, and fought in the defence of Antwerp. Just as things were hotting up there, Admiralty recalled the squadron. " Dare-devil " Samson—as he had come to be known—cursed his luck and prayed for fog so that he could stay in this growingly intense theatre of war.

There was no fog and he and his pilots set out for home. Over Dunkerque, one of the planes got into difficulties, spun down, crash-landed in a field. Samson could see very well that the pilot was unharmed, but he ordered the whole squadron to go to his aid. And once on the ground he managed to find a number of mysterious mechanical defects in other aircraft which would delay them here—keep them all, as he put it, " in business."

Over the next few weeks he continued to make excuses to Admiralty for his delay in leaving France, until Whitehall —perhaps unwilling to battle with Samson as well as the Germans—agreed to keep him at Dunkerque for operations against Zeppelins.

With the Allied Armies in retreat, there were opportunities in plenty for a man of Samson's vigour and ingenuity. And not all were in the air. For instance, with his brother, Felix, he built up a squad of motor cars armed with machine-guns—the first armoured cars in history. And he personally led them in battle against German cavalry units.

In the air he was equally active, attacking Zeppelin hangars and submarine bases at Zeebrugge and Ostend. He drove himself mercilessly, seemed hardly to sleep. Then he was switched with his squadron to the Dardanelles.

His base at Kephalo Point, on the island of Imbros, was particularly vulnerable to Turkish air attack. One night, just before the regular midnight raid on Kephalo, Samson ordered his squadron to load up and be ready to take off when the Turks drew near. The pilots thought that they were merely getting their planes out of the way of disaster, but Samson led them to Chanak, the Turks' aerodrome.

The Turkish ground crews thought the British squadron was their own, returning from the raid on Kephalo, and obligingly lit their landing flares. Down swept Samson, leading his force in a fierce, low-level strafing and bombing run that left the airfield a pitted, smoking ruin. After that, the Turks left the British flyers in peace at nights.

In 1917, after a spell as commander of the seaplane carrier *Ben-My-Chree*, Samson returned to England and was given an important but irksome desk job. After a few months he made such a nuisance of himself that his superiors once more gave in, let him return to active duty. For the remaining months of the war he was busy flying defensive patrols, day and night, up and down the coast from Yarmouth Air Station—all the time improving techniques, submitting reports on various tactical and operational experiments, suggesting new methods and devices and training systems and weapons. . . .

After the war he was transferred to the newly-formed Royal Air Force, given the high rank of Air Commodore and stationed at Uxbridge, a few miles from London. It was there that a heart complaint, developed in the strenuous days of the war, became serious. Samson, the Navy's strong man, had burnt himself out. He died in 1931.

A prophetically far-sighted officer, a brilliant pilot and totally brave, Charles Rumney Samson is remembered as " the man who gave the Navy wings." Of his many contributions to naval aviation, undoubtedly the most important was his dream of a new kind of vessel carrying fighters, " a floating aerodrome." His incredible take-offs from *Africa* and *Hibernia* perhaps did not convince all the Sea Lords that this idea was feasible, but they did set a number of expert minds, in the backrooms of Admiralty and the great ship-building firms, to work on this problem, and after many years this activity produced the forerunner of the modern aircraft carrier—nowadays rated more effective than any battleship.

And Samson lived to see this work in progress. After his successful take-offs, he had planned to attempt landings —but this demanded a somewhat larger deck area, and no suitable ship was available. Then came the war, and he put the idea out of his mind for the duration—and consequently was beaten to it. For in 1917 another naval pilot, Commander F. H. Dunning, became the first man to land an aircraft on a ship.

Dunning was very different in character from Samson. Strong too, but in a slower, subtler way. Gentle of voice and manners, a methodical and skilful airman, he had served with quiet distinction through the first three years of the war. He knew of Samson's theories, was deeply impressed by the strategic implications. Almost diffidently, in the early summer of 1917 he put forward his startling proposal: could he have permission to land his plane, a Sopwith Pup, on the fo'c'sle of H.M.S. *Furious*?

" Impossible—suicidal—a pointless stunt. . . ." These reactions from Admiralty were strangely similar to those which had greeted Samson's first request, five years before, to " borrow " the *Africa*. But now there were a few progressive minds, impressed by the rapid development of the aeroplane as a fighting machine, and by its success in France, and uncomfortably aware that in the near future capital ships would have to be protected by an " air umbrella." Various schemes based on Samson's proposals had been held up for lack of funds; if it could be proved that a modern fighter could land safely on a ship's deck, some of the sceptics might be won over and money made available.

So the few supporters of the Samson-Dunning school of thought, seizing their chance, fought hard to get permission for the attempt. And by the end of July, after many violent verbal battles behind locked doors in Whitehall, they won.

On 2nd August, 1917, Dunning's little Pup hovered like an uncertain, grumbling bee over the *Furious*. While he worked out his approach path, hundreds of anxious eyes followed him and tension on the ship mounted to such a pitch that some of the officers asked the captain to cancel the bid, and turn out of wind. Sternly the captain refused —he was under orders from Admiralty; his task was to " give this young maniac full facilities to kill himself."

The methodical, experienced Dunning, having carefully surveyed his objective and worked out every action beforehand in his mind, brought the Pup down with its nose high and plenty of power, in a beautifully steady approach, until his wheels were two or three feet above the after edge of the frighteningly short fo'c'sle. Then he closed the throttle, held the stick fully back against his taut diaphragm. The aircraft stalled, dropped like a stone, flopped down in a perfect three-point landing. It stopped with yards to spare.

The sceptics at the Admiralty were shaken. The air-minded few launched an all-out argumentative attack, and at last it was agreed that experiments should continue and that money should be provided for investigating the possibility of designing " a sea-going aerodrome." The future of the Navy's air branch, and the coming of the great aircraft carriers envisaged so long ago by " Daredevil " Samson, were thus finally assured.

On 7th August—five days later—Dunning made his second attempt to land on Furious. This time he was watched by several experts, scientists and Admiralty chiefs.

His approach was perfect, down to the last few feet. But when he cut the throttle and hauled the stick back, he was a shade too high. At first the Pup fell vertically as before, but then one wing began to drop, so that he came down hard on one wheel. The plane bounced, rocked crazily, swung to one side, careered across the deck and over the side, into the sea. And sank at once.

Dunning, strapped in his cockpit, went down with her. In just five days this quiet, methodical, brave airman had written his name in triumph and tragedy on the honours roll of Britain's air pioneers.

But Dunning's death spoilt nothing—the matter had already been settled, he had proved once that it could be done. Like Samson, he had had to use as his " aerodrome " a standard ship of the line, never intended for such exotic service. A few more yards of deck, or a sturdy crash-barrier, would have saved him. By his sacrifice, he had emphasised the needs ; he had shown that a vessel specially designed to despatch and receive aircraft could greatly reduce the very dangers which had destroyed him.

When Samson was told of Dunning's fate, somehow he felt responsible. Deeply moved, he said : " Somebody had to do it, but it was really up to me. Now they *must* see the whole idea is practical . . . now they *must* build us what we need ! "

And throughout the years, up until his death, he kept up a valuable correspondence with the designers of the first aircraft carriers, suggesting modifications and additional safety devices—making sure that the Admiralty kept faith with his old colleague Dunning.

CHAPTER THREE

KNIGHT OF THE SILVER CUPS

CAPTAIN OSWALD Boelcke was drawn and aching with tiredness. In the last few weeks he had covered thousands of miles, visiting fighter stations, training fields and air headquarters throughout Germany and France, testing and selecting young pilots for the new, special wing which the Kaiser's experts had ordered him to form. Now, on his way back from the Eastern Front, drooping eyelids and stiffening limbs had forced him to land at this remote bomber base at Kovel.

He got a tremendous welcome in the officers' mess. The pilots of this squadron of two-seater bombers, stuck out here in aviator's " Siberia " in the iron-hard winter of 1915-16, detested their work—raids on the Russians, who had no air protection at all—and thought they saw in Boelcke a chance to escape, to transfer to fighters and go to France where " the real war " was being fought and great personal glory could be won. But he told them bluntly : " I'm sorry, gentlemen, the new wing is as good as complete. I'm not here to find candidates—simply to beg a meal and a bed for the night." And as soon as he had eaten he excused himself, thanked them for their hospitality, and went to the room they had given him.

He took off his tunic, and was sitting on the edge of the bed pulling off his boots when there came a short, sharp knock on the door. He groaned, called wearily : " Come in." A tall, slender, very straight and immaculate young officer entered, clicked his heels. On the bare floorboards the scrape and thud of the leather seemed extraordinarily loud.

"Good evening, sir," said the young man, and his voice was quick, confident, undoubtedly affected. "I'm Richthofen. You may remember—we met on a train some months ago." Vaguely, very vaguely, Boelcke remembered, and he gave him a tired smile and a nod.

"Yes, of course. How nice to see you again, Richthofen. Were you in the mess? I'm sorry if I didn't recognise you—the fact is, I'm about all in."

"That's quite all right, sir. I *was* in the mess, but I kept out of the way—I didn't feel like bothering you there. With all the others. . . ."

Boelcke sighed, let his head fall forward, peering at the floorboards between his boots.

"All right," he said, "so you've come to bother me now—you've waited to get me alone, eh? Very enterprising, but I'm afraid the answer's still the same. I don't need any more pilots, and if I did I shouldn't look for them in a bomber squadron."

"But I have experience on scouts and fighters—in France, before I came here. I have always known that I'm not temperamentally suited to bomber operations. If you would only consider me, sir, look at my record . . ."

"I'm sorry, Richthofen. I've picked my men." Boelcke yawned, went on with the job of removing his boots. But his visitor showed no signs of leaving.

"May I ask a question, Captain?" Boelcke nodded, without looking up. "What do you consider is the most important qualification of the fighter pilot?"

"Marksmanship," Boelcke replied without a moment's hesitation. "A man may be a wonderful flyer, and full of courage, but if he can't shoot straight it's a waste of time putting him in a plane."

" I was hoping you'd say that, sir ! " The heels clicked again, like some heavy bolt slamming home. " I have the honour to report that I am a crackshot, sir, with any weapon, from a revolver to a machine-gun. I spend hours shooting, every day. As a matter of fact, I supplied your dinner to-night—wood pigeon. Yesterday it was venison. This squadron never has to buy meat or poultry."

The Captain looked up, chuckled softly ; Richthofen was standing straight as a bayonet, chin jutting high, his lean, aristocratic face flushed with pride. This youngster was vain and cocksure, but if he really kept the mess provided with fresh meat, then he must be a very fine shot indeed.

" Good for you," Boelcke said. " I'll remember that, and if there are any vacancies in the future I certainly will consider you."

" While you're here, sir, will you not look at my official service record ? It's in the commander's office."

" All right, I'll look at your record. In the morning, before I leave."

" Thank you, Captain." A stiff, Prussian bow as he backed to the door. " While you're going through it, I'll see if I can bag you a brace of pheasants to take back with you. Good night, sir."

The first thing Boelcke realised, as he began to read through the young officer's personal record file early next morning, was that Richthofen could never have seen this himself—if he had, he certainly wouldn't have let it get into the hands of anyone he wanted to impress ! Officers' official records were supposed to be confidential, of course

—that is, for the eyes of unit commanders and headquarters " brass " only—but in time of war paper-work
was not taken too seriously, the files were not guarded
strictly and most pilots had little difficulty in getting hold
of them, finding out how they had been rated and reported
by instructors and flight commanders right through their
careers. But Richthofen, no doubt confident that his file
did him credit, probably hadn't bothered to sneak a look.

It was an intriguing document. He had been in trouble
frequently, mostly for insubordination. He was described
by former commanders variously—as " headstrong,"
" over-confident," " disrespectful," but nearly all the
contributors agreed, if grudgingly, that he was highly,
unfailingly enthusiastic, and had great physical courage
and stamina. One or two assessments—which struck
Boelcke as perhaps more shrewd and thorough than the
rest—clearly suggested that this son of an old and noble
family was an incurable romantic, terribly aware of the
chivalrous traditions of his class, obsessed by a wild sense
of destiny and fired by ambitions which were totally
unjustified by his very ordinary capabilities.

Not surprisingly, he had started the war as a dashing,
sabre-swinging cavalry officer. Reading between the lines,
it wasn't difficult to see that it had taken him some months
to face reality—to see that his dreams of galloping glory
belonged in another age, that there was little scope for
cavalry in the muddy drudgery of 1914 and trench warfare.
But once he saw this, obviously he had decided immediately
that to seek his radiant destiny he must enter the new list
of the twentieth century—the air.

At first his regiment would not release him, but his
persistence wore down opposition and in May, 1915, he
forsook saddle for cockpit. But training schools for pilots

(*above*) Albatross C.111,s of the Richtofen " Flying Circus." With a top speed of 120 m.p.h., the Albatross was one of the best German fighters, and it destroyed 368 Allied aircraft in the disastrous month of April 1917. Richtofen's famous all-red machine is third from the camera.
(*Photo: Maurice Allward.*)

(*right*) Baron Manfred von Richtofen, "The Red Knight of Germany," had destroyed over 80 allied aircraft when he was killed in action in 1918. (*Photo: Imperial War Museum.*)

(*left*) S.E.5A Scouts of No. 85 Squadron in France, 1918. Powered by a 200 h.p. Hispano or Wolseley Viper engine, they had a top speed of 132 m.p.h.
(*Photo: Maurice Allward.*)

(*below*) Sopwith Camel, greatest British fighting scout of World War I. With a top speed of 115 m.p.h. and manœuvrability which became legend, it destroyed 1,294 enemy aircraft.
(*Photo: Hawker Aircraft.*)

were full; he was made an observer, and served on operations in France.

After a few months he had applied for pilot training, and when this was refused apparently persuaded his own pilot to teach him. But for all his confidence and enthusiasm, according to the reports of this reluctant instructor, Richthofen proved a poor student. His touch on the controls was described as "heavy-handed," his judgment of height and distance was "uncertain" and he had a frightening lack of co-ordination. After many hours of dual instruction, suddenly he seemed to improve—to get the knack of it all. On an October afternoon he took off for his first solo flight. Coming in to land he let his speed get too low, the nose too high. The aircraft went into a spin and crashed. The accident report showed the machine was destroyed, but Richthofen was only bruised and shaken and was fit for normal duties as observer within a few hours.

Boelcke's guess was that after this accident Richthofen's pilot had refused to give him any further instruction, for the file contained no more progress reports by him. But Richthofen must have continued to practise alone, and made a successful solo flight without authority, for only a few weeks later he entered the normal examination for pilots, competing against officers, who had been through the full, official training course. He failed—disastrously. Yet nothing could destroy his simple faith in his destiny; he continued his secret, solitary practice, entered the examination again a few weeks later and scraped through with scant marks to spare. His flying had improved only slightly, but his examiners this time took more interest in theoretical and technical matters and were impressed by his grasp of aero-engineering and maintenance, armaments, signalling procedure and air tactics. Obviously he had been studying very hard.

The file contained a letter written by Richthofen on the day he was informed that he had passed the examination. Doubtless and audacious as a prophet, he requested to be posted to a fighter squadron—though at that time only the most skilful aircraft-handlers were assigned to the fast, light and sensitive single-seater machines. Richthofen was given a sturdy, two-seater observation plane.

After that he had served for some weeks quietly, without distinction, spotting for the artillery and reconnoitring British and French rear lines and supply routes. It was noted that under fire he remained utterly unperturbed, but the standard of his flying was still below average.

Then somehow, persistent as the seasons, he had talked a senior officer into " pulling strings " and getting him transferred to a fighter squadron. At last glory was within his grasp, in a matter of weeks or months he would be an ace ; to celebrate his success in advance, he threw a lavish farewell party for his friends at the observation squadron mess.

He had lasted less than fourteen days on fighters. After wrecking two machines, and very nearly colliding in mid-air with his squadron commander, he was swiftly transferred back to larger, slower planes—this time a bomber squadron stationed on the Eastern Front. At Kovel. And he had remained here, complaining and scheming and not very popular, ever since.

Boelcke was about to replace the file in the commander's cupboard when a loose sheet of paper fell out. He stooped, retrieved it, glanced at the writing. It was a letter written by Richthofen during his time with the observation squadron, and in it he reported " a private experiment " and claimed the destruction of two Allied fighters behind the enemy lines. German observation planes at that stage were usually unarmed, or else equipped with only a single, antiquated and ineffective gun mounted on a scarf-ring round the observer's cockpit. Boelcke could not recall ever having heard of one destroying an enemy fighter. He read on, intrigued but sceptical.

The letter described in some detail, how Richthofen had found a way to rig a Spandau machine-gun on the upper wing of the observation plane, and run a cable from its trigger to his cockpit. Attacked on a long-distance patrol, he said he had shot down two fighters. Though his observer and the crew of an accompanying plane added signed statements that they had witnessed this engagement, it seemed that Richthofen's claim had not been allowed—his superiors simply hadn't believed him. But the signature of one of the witnesses now caught Boelcke's eye—a personal friend, whom he knew to be a man of unquestionable honour. If this were true—if Richthofen had managed to bag two small, fast fighters with a crude contraption like that—then he must be a truly wonderful marksman, one of the best shots in the German forces !

As if to confirm this idea, as the Captain left the commander's office a tall figure came out of the thick woods beyond the airfield's boundary. He walked stiffly, almost a strut; and he was carrying a sporting gun—and three brace of pheasants.

Watching him approach, Boelcke thought of the task ahead for his new, special wing of fighters, and wondered if this strange, stiff young dandy, vain yet courageous, ludicrously ambitious yet loyal and eager—a sort of Don Quixote of the skies—could possibly fit in after all. He was certainly an unusual and colourful personality, and that was important; one couldn't help admiring his earnestness and persistence; and if he was half as good a shot as his record indicated, and as he himself so readily declared, and as those six pheasants testified——?

Boelcke decided to take a chance. He would take Richthofen back with him. On trial. If he didn't fit in, he'd find himself back on bombers or scouts faster than he could click those polished heels.

The other pilots, hand-picked from the finest units of Germany's air force, literally made rings round Richthofen in the practise dog-fights which were part of the new wing's exacting training programme. Despite his hundreds of hours of experience, he was not by any stretch of the imagination a natural flyer; he was still clumsy, heavy-handed in manœuvres, and his landings were shocking, often downright dangerous.

But no one worked harder, tried harder, studied longer or displayed more coolness under long, severe strain.

To get his " cubs " used to the speed and durability of their new Albatross biplane fighters, Boelcke used to take the whole wing up in a loose formation to about 15,000 feet then suddenly, without warning, slam his stick forward, open his throttle and dive, full out, to 1,000 feet. In this, Richthofen was always a poor last—slow to react to his leader's sudden descent, liable to lose sight of the others on his way down and pull out either too early or dangerously late. And on other exercises he was little better.

But when it came to gunnery he was the star performer. And so vain, so infuriatingly sarcastic about the others, that he encouraged every man on the squadron to work hard and improve his shooting " just for the pleasure of beating him, just once. . . ."

By the beginning of September they were ready. Boelcke explained to them their vital task—kept secret up till now for security reasons. In the past, the German air policy had laid emphasis on defence ; the role of the fighters was to protect artillery and troops from air attack, sometimes to escort their bomber colleagues, and to maintain standing patrols over key positions, supply depots and ammunition dumps. In other words, unlike the British fighters, they did not seek battle—they fought only when called upon.

" Now, after more than two years of war, we are changing our tactics," he said. " We are no longer a purely defensive force—we are going over to the offensive, hitting wherever we can, as hard as we can. And this wing, as a new and specially created unit, will open this offensive."

The pilots cheered—too long had the swashbuckling British enjoyed the advantage of picking the time and place of battle between forces of fighters ! Now the Tommies were due for some surprises—they'd find themselves rousted out at odd hours to meet the challenge of a crack German unit hungry for combat !

The man who cheered loudest was Richthofen ; in this new policy of aggression he saw at last the long-sought opportunity which would bring him fame and glory.

The British formation of scout-bombers flew unhurriedly in a wide circle over their own base. In the distance, glinting in the September sun, they could see the German planes—apparently patrolling their " beat " as usual, high above their army's trenches and heavy batteries. Plenty of time ; Jerry never moved until he was attacked. The British could climb, leisurely survey the situation, then simply fly round the obstacle.

And then, almost before the shocked British pilots

realised it, the Germans were sweeping down across no-man's-land in tight, attacking formation; thirteen sleek and graceful Albatrosses. Too late, frantic hands opened throttles, pulled back on the sticks—there was no time to climb to meet this unexpected assault; for once the Germans were going to have the advantage of altitude.

Boelcke, leading his " cubs," had stationed Richthofen next to his own plane, intending to keep an eye on him if he could. But as they sliced down on the British pack, spreading out in order to pick their victims, the ex-bomber pilot with the " shaky " flying record seemed to draw out ahead of his comrades, plunge in first and fasten on to a large, two-seater Vickers F.E.

At the controls of the F.E. was Flight-Lieutenant L.B.F. Morris; in the observer's seat, Lieutenant T. Rees. Rees had a big Lewis gun mounted on a turntable pivot, and Morris had another fixed to the fuselage, firing forward through the propeller arc and fitted with the new Constantinescu synchronisation device which ensured that the bullets did not hit the spinning blades. Both airmen were " veterans " of the Royal Flying Corps, and Rees had a proud reputation for marksmanship.

Richthofen closed to fifty yards, opened fire with his twin Spandaus. Rees retaliated, and Richthofen was forced to dive out of range. He came back, climbing steeply to above and behind the British plane. Rees opened up again. Some of his bullets were very near; at any moment a stream of them could hit home. Richthofen banked into a cloud, circled and prepared to come in to the attack for the third time—at a lower level. Morris was now flying the F.E. straight and level, no doubt thinking the German had been beaten off for good, and for the moment there was no need to twist and turn evasively.

Boelcke had taught Richthofen and the other "cubs" about a certain "blind spot"—a small approach angle which could be covered neither by an F.E. pilot nor the observer. Richthofen now went for this spot. And Morris flew on, unaware that his super-persistent foe lurked still under his tail.

Throttle wide open, Richthofen rose steeply towards the smooth, red belly of the F.E. Thirty yards from his target his Spandaus rattled out. As he came up and passed to one side of his victim, he noticed that the propeller had stopped. The pilot had been hit. The released controls reared and bucked, the F.E. side-slipped, fell away.

Richthofen followed it down. He saw that the observer was also slumped in his seat. Unguided, the plane crossed no-man's-land, passed over the German lines. Then, as it neared the ground, Morris regained consciousness, straightened out and made a good landing. Richthofen, the unscathed victor, brought his Albatross down in the same field—and, clumsy as ever, almost smashed it!

He ran to the British plane and helped to lift Morris and Rees out; minutes later they died on the way to a hospital. Sadly he flew back to his airfield. There, the sadness lifted, he smirked and strutted, flushed with victory.

Boelcke's "cubs" had acquitted themselves well; four other pilots had scored kills in the battle. There was champagne in the mess and to Richthofen and each of the other four a delighted Boelcke presented a silver tankard.

But Richthofen, now completely sure of himself, felt this did not mark the victory—the start of his true, lustrous career—with enough emphasis. So he wrote to a Berlin jeweller and ordered a silver cup, two inches high and inscribed: "1 Vickers 17.9.16." He announced that he intended to have a cup made for each of his future kills.

By 1918, Richthofen—" The Red Knight of Germany," in a scarlet-painted plane—had shot down eighty machines. But he had only sixty cups: the jeweller in luxury-starved Germany had run out of silver!

Those silver cups perhaps provide us with the most revealing clue to the personality of Captain Baron Manfred von Richthofen. Without doubt he was inordinately vain, and revelled in self-glorification. As the tally of his " kills " mounted, he held aloof from his colleagues and became a tough, silent commander when later he formed his own wing—a sixty-strong " circus " of fighters. He remained a clumsy pilot—and an incredibly brilliant marksman. His courage, his love of flying and his passionate loyalty never diminished, but he lost his old romantic idea of chivalry—the sort of impulse which had led him down to try to help his early victims, Morris and Rees.

He met his death in April, 1918, it is said, while attacking a young pilot whose guns had jammed. He failed to notice another British fighter, getting on to his own tail. It was piloted by a very able Canadian aviator, Captain Roy Brown.

A short burst of machine-gun fire. The Baron's red-painted plane reared, dipped out of control, crash-landed behind the Allied lines.

Richthofen, the crackshot, who always told his pilots " Never shoot for the plane—shoot at the man," was found slumped in his cockpit. Shot through the chest.

CHAPTER FOUR

STARS OF NO-MAN'S-SKY

Tongues of orange and white fire lashed the night sky and the crash of exploding shells rocked several miles of Allied trenches. Along the front line troops huddled together in the mud and wondered if this were just another of the regular probings to test Allied opposition, or the overture to a mass attack on the morrow.

It was 1917. A time of terrible uncertainty; a time when the tide of war on the Western Front could be changed by one sustained German break-through.

After perhaps an hour, there came a pause in the barrage. At a Royal Flying Corps airfield behind the lines, in the sudden silence a violin was heard playing a slow, wistful melody. It seemed like a tiny voice crying out for peace amid the muddy, smoky destruction.

An enemy flare climbed slowly above no-man's-land and its pale, pulsing light silhouetted the musician, sitting outside a tent. A slim, boyish figure, with his head thoughtfully tilted to catch the mood of his own strange, sweet music. Then the flare died and the German big guns again took up the harsh symphony of war.

Nineteen-year-old Albert Ball closed his eyes, tried not to listen to the guns, continued to play his violin. He hated war.

To many of the other, older pilots it was a mystery that this sensitive lad from a well-to-do home in Nottingham had volunteered to fly. Deeply religious, he had in his eyes the look of the early Christian fanatic. And yet it was a fact that he was proving himself a natural flyer and fearless fighter.

Yes, a strange mixture, Albert Ball. Near his tent out there in France stood his Nieuport—the little one-seater " skin-and-bone " plane which was showing itself such a reliable war machine. And on the other side of the tent, picked out in the mud, was a small garden, fresh with early spring flowers. Both the plane and the garden Ball tended with loving care. Both were part of his life—along with his music.

The Royal Flying Corps had suffered heavy losses in the winter just gone. In four bitter months over the Somme, 867 airmen had died. The average life of a pilot was three weeks when Ball arrived in France to join No. 13 Squadron.

At first he had flown in a two-seater B.E.2 and was engaged on artillery observation. But even in this slow and cumbersome craft he managed to shoot down two Germans. He was transferred to No. 11 Squadron, equipped with the speedier Nieuport.

Among his gay, wild young comrades, Ball was a man apart. He was almost oppressively quiet in the mess ; he never went " out on the spree " with the others. He wrote home regularly, but not about the war ; his letters to his father were full of his little garden, and invariably ended with requests for more seeds and plants.

But with the more experienced pilots he would often spend hours—asking questions, talking technicalities and tactics. He was a passionate admirer of the two superb French aces, René Fonck and Charles Nungesser. (Fonck's total of kills reached 75, Nungesser's 45. Both survived, but in May, 1927, Nungesser was lost on an attempted Atlantic flight.)

As in the mess, Ball preferred to be alone in the air. He never wore goggles or a helmet—" I like to feel the wind in my hair," he explained half-apologetically.

Within weeks of joining the squadron he had conceived and perfected perhaps the most dangerous, but most effective technique yet known in aerial warfare.

It was generally accepted that if an enemy plane got above and behind a pilot then nine times out of ten the pilot could not shake it off. But Ball would go out of his way to allow a German to get on his tail. Then with his uncanny ability to sense the instant when the enemy was about to open fire he would turn away sharply and, in a special, brilliant manœuvre he had worked out, with amazing swiftness come up under the other plane and attack in the " blind spot."

As impressive to his comrades was his steel-nerved method of flying head-on against a German, calling his bluff and forcing him to turn away at the last moment. That left the German plane vulnerable for perhaps a second —enough time for Ball, a crackshot, to send home a deadly burst of bullets. Ball's amazing marksmanship was not entirely a gift—on the ground he drilled with rifle and revolver, hour after hour, keeping his eye true. And almost always he supervised the servicing of his plane's armament.

Such methods quickly gained for the young officer a high reputation, and when he went to 56 Squadron even established aces like Rhys-Davies and Major J. B. McCudden became admirers of this strange, quiet youth. His senior officers, noting his unusual talent as a lone wolf, gave him what amounted to a " roving commission." And nobody plagued him to join in mess parties at nights— he could stay out in the moonlight, alone, with his violin.

During this period he went out on solitary patrol one

day and met two German Albatrosses. He dived to the attack and inflicted damage on one of the planes. But before he could turn his attention to the second machine, he ran out of ammunition. The Albatrosses took this chance to turn tail and flee. Ball followed—keeping up his attack with his revolver !

He continued this strange pursuit until the enemy reached their own airfield, and then he scribbled a note on the little pad strapped to his thigh, swooped low and dropped it on the grass. The note challenged the two Albatrosses to a new battle with him at first light of dawn.

Next morning Ball, his hair streaming in the wind, set off for the rendezvous, alone. He arrived in time to see his two adversaries of the previous day circling slowly, reluctantly. He flew towards the nearer one, intending to use his head-on technique—a shrewd tactic against such nervous foes. He was closing fast when machine-gun bullets hosed all round him.

He pulled up and turned tightly, immediately saw that three other planes had joined the attack, diving from the cover of a cloud patch. He was trapped. Ball was famous even to the enemy, and they were not letting a small thing like chivalry stand in the way of such a prize of war. So it was five-to-one against him !

The Germans had planned their tactics well : every time the British pilot tried to close and pick off one of them, all five kept swerving out of his range. Three worked their way back to cut off his line of retreat, while the other two teased him into chasing them further into German-held territory. Ball, firing at long range, for the second time in less than twenty-four hours ran out of ammunition.

The Germans soon discovered this, and the two planes he had chased turned to face him—to finish him off. They opened fire together, and after two short bursts the British plane fell into a steep, tight spin. As the two attacking Germans followed it down, their three waiting companions waggled their wings to signal victory and flew off with the news—the British ace was about to crash far behind the German lines.

But Ball had not been hit, he was only feigning. Nearing the ground, he eased out of the spin, straightened his plane slightly, just sufficiently to make a landing—an awkward, lurching landing that appeared to be a fluke, or at best the last effort of a dying pilot. It was a brilliant display of aircraft handling—a convincing piece of acting. As the plane stopped, he slumped forward, kept still.

The two Germans, who had followed him down, landed in the same field, leapt from their machines. They were running to examine their prize when Ball's slumped figure suddenly came to life. He opened his throttle. The fighter trundled forward, gathered speed, lifted just over their heads. Before the Germans could get back to their own cockpits and follow, Ball was a diminishing speck—scudding at low level back towards the Allied lines.

Very rarely did Ball—soon made a captain—fly with other pilots, but on 17th May, 1917, he was one of eleven fighter men who set out " to look for trouble." By that time the quiet, flower-loving, violin-playing youth had shot down forty enemy machines and been awarded the Distinguished Service Order (with two bars) and the Military Cross.

A cold day, with a hard brightness. Great puffs of cloud sailed high above the bevy of British machines. From the distance tiny specks expanded suddenly into an armada of Albatrosses. The British patrol opened throttles and tore into the enemy formation.

In the first minute of the battle Ball was seen to climb into a cloud in pursuit of a fleeing German. When the dog-fight broke up, and the British pilots re-formed and turned for home, there was no sign of him. That night the airfield still waited, hoping to hear a drone in the darkness—perhaps he had made a forced landing, or put down at another base. . . . But dawn came, and it was clear that Albert Ball would never return. The exact manner of his death remains a mystery to this day.

He was posthumously awarded the Victoria Cross.

Ball's example—his innovations, his unflagging courage and constant drilling—had fired the imagination of another young pilot—a very different personality.

Edward (Micky) Mannock was the son of a regular soldier, one of a large family. He had been handicapped by poverty, lack of education and bad eyesight. At twelve he had been sent out to work as a greengrocer's boy.

After that there had been various, unpromising jobs before, full of determination to gain some sort of security, he packed up and went to seek his fortune in Turkey. He arrived just in time to find that country at war with Britain ! At once he was interned, but after a few months, largely because of his defective eyesight, he was sent home with a batch of exchanged prisoners.

Immediately, he joined a Royal Army Medical Corps unit, and later got a commission in the Royal Engineers. In France he used to lie in the mud-choked trenches, watching Albert Ball and the other heroes of the sky fly out to another day of high-speed action in the wide, clear blue. To him, despite the high casualty rate in pilots, theirs was a life infinitely to be preferred to the sluggish, soggy routine of a " sapper."

By now one of his eyes had returned to normal as a result

of treatment by a gifted Army doctor, but the other was still defective—almost useless, in fact. And, of course, top grading in eyesight was essential for flyers. Even so, Micky Mannock applied for a transfer to the Flying Corps.

At his medical examination he had to read letters on a test card with one eye at a time—the other being covered by the examiner. He began with his good eye, and found no difficulty. Then came an enormous stroke of luck. The doctor was called away for a few moments. And in those moments Mannock stared hard at the card with his good eye, managed to memorise all the letters. The doctor returned, and after the " reading " passed the useless eye as top grade!

In training he showed no great promise, qualified with average gradings and was sent to fighters.

On his first squadron he came under the influence of one of Albert Ball's old comrades, the ace " Mac " McCudden.

McCudden liked the highly-strung, argumentative young man—and indeed felt sorry for him, for Micky had strong likes and dislikes and an unfortunate way of upsetting people, losing friends. Through many feuds and sulks, McCudden stuck by him—perhaps realising that Mannock's tough childhood had left him with a feeling of inferiority and an unreasonable suspicion of the motives of others.

A real test of their friendship came after some operational flights when Mannock—the man who was always talking of his relish for adventure and action—seemed to temper his boldness with perhaps a little too much " reliable judgment." His seniors began to doubt whether he had the fibre of a pilot. In the mess his comrades hinted broadly that the newcomer talked big, but had " cold feet."

McCudden alone did not doubt Mannock; he took him aside, tried to find out the reason for the youngster's apparent failure to press home his attacks and make what appeared simple " kills." But Mannock sulked, would say nothing.

So McCudden watched him closely on the next patrol and suddenly, in the middle of a dog-fight, discovered Mannock's weakness—he was a shockingly poor marksman ! Back at the airfield he ordered Mannock out for machine-gun practice on the range, and in a matter of minutes found out the secret of Mannock's defective eyesight.

The older pilot was uncertain what to do for the best— if he reported his discovery, Mannock would be permanently grounded ; on the other hand, was it right to let a man go on flying when he was not fully fit, when he could not protect himself properly ? And was it fair to the rest of the squadron ?

In the end he decided to postpone a decision—to wait a little and see whether, with practice, the youngster could improve his shooting. Mannock was ready to work till he dropped, and day after day they spent hours on the range. Slowly, together they evolved a method by which Mannock corrected for his defective eye, making allowance for it in aiming—and to the astonishment of both he became a first class shot !

He worked just as hard to improve his flying, taking off alone between operational flights to practise the difficult and dangerous aerobatic manœuvres introduced by the legendary lone-wolf Ball, and the experienced, patient McCudden. Very soon his doubting messmates noted the change ; in a matter of a few months " Cold Feet " Mannock became " Wild Micky " or "Mad Mannock," and his bag of " kills " mounted steadily.

The sulkiness, the lingering sense of inferiority and

(*above*) Capt. Albert Ball, V.C., D.S.O. and 2 bars, M.C., in the cockpit of his S.E.5 Fighter. He was killed in action over the German lines on May 7th, 1917.

(*below*) Capt. W. A. Bishop, V.C., D.S.O., M.C. When this photograph was taken (6th August 1917) he had 37 German aircraft to his credit.

(*Photos: Imperial War Museum.*)

(*above*) Major J. B. " Mac " McCudden, V.C., D.S.O., M.C., M.M. in an S.E.5. Noted for steadiness, he won 58 victories.

(*left*) Major " Micky " Mannock, V.C., D.S.O., and 2 bars, M.C. and bar, at St. Omer, June 1918. " The Mad Major," who bluffed his way into the Royal Flying Corps despite defective vision, was officially credited with 73 " kills."

(*Photos: Imperial War Museum.*)

defensive truculence, left him as his confidence grew. At last the ex-greengrocer's boy had found " some sort of security "—it didn't matter to him that to hold on to it he had to place his life in jeopardy every day. He became a cheerful, popular figure in the mess, and displayed immense patience with the less experienced pilots—the same sort of patience that McCudden had shown to him. And he was the instigator and leading figure of countless wild squadron parties.

With no fewer than 73 " kills " to his official credit, he was awarded the Victoria Cross. To thousands in the trenches—on both sides of no-man's-land—he was referred to now simply as " the mad Major." After an air battle, he had a habit of swooping down and skimming along the Allied lines—where he himself had spent many miserable months—waggling his wings and waving to the troops. The soldiers looked forward to his visits, cheered and waved back—it gave them fresh heart to know they had this great flyer on their side, a man who understood their grimmer, dirtier, less personal war here on the ground, and who thought about them enough to drop in now and then.

Occasionally, to provide a diversion for the weary, muddy infantrymen, Mannock would put on a display of aerobatics, rolling and looping and spinning his plane, pulling out scant feet above the parapets. Once or twice, where no-man's-land was particularly narrow, Germans following his crazy progress from the other side would open fire on the stunting plane. Then the Mad Major was apt to roar across and, to the delight of the watching Tommies, " beat up " the enemy positions, diving so low that the Germans were forced to abandon their guns and lie flat on their faces in the mire.

On the night of 26th July, 1918—just four months before

the end of the war—Mannock was holding one of his parties at the airfield's mess. Donald Inglis, a young New Zealander who had joined the squadron only a few days before, was standing on one side, a little shy, feeling a bit out of things. Mannock came up, slapped his shoulder.

" Cheer up, Don! What's the matter—don't you like it here ? "

" I like it fine, sir," Inglis said with a grin. " But I'll like it better once I've broken my duck and bagged myself a Hun."

" What ?—haven't you got one yet ? Well now, soon put that right! Come up with me in the morning, I'll show you a good hunting ground. Jerry's been sending a two-seater job over to scout this sector every morning, same time to the minute. Up till now I haven't bothered with him, but he's getting too cocksure, coming in very low —taking advantage of our good nature. He's yours, Don. Come with me at dawn and I'll set him up for you."

A few hours later, while the other pilots were still asleep, the fledgling Inglis and the veteran Mannock took off into a salmon dawn. Over the Allied front line, just as Mannock had predicted, they spotted the German—circling, insolently low. Together they dived on him. Mannock pulled ahead, and a little off to one side, neatly drawing the enemy's fire and forcing him to turn his back on Inglis.

Inglis, in his excitement, came up so fast on the slower scout-plane that he almost collided with its tail. He steadied himself, opened fire. The German staggered under the short-range blast, keeled over, crashed in no-man's-land in a big gout of flame.

Inglis and Mannock circled the wreck, then set course for base and breakfast. They were flying at about two hundred feet, nearer to the German lines than their own.

Below—more as an act of defiance than in real hope—enemy infantrymen sniped at them with rifles. The Mad Major did not deign to take the slightest notice.

They were almost out of range of the small-arms fire when Inglis, glancing over at Mannock, saw flames begin to lick out of the leader's cowling. He waved, pointed frantically, then Mannock seemed to straighten in his cockpit, kick his rudder hard, struggle with the controls. Down went the crippled plane's nose, and now the flames gushed from it, consuming wings and fuselage even as it fell into a spin. The blazing wreck turned twice, and smote the ground as little more than a ball of fire.

Inglis knew Mannock could not have lived in that inferno—he was probably dead before he hit the churned mud of the battleground where, many months and more than seventy victories ago, he had lain and craned his neck to watch, and to envy, the flashing wings of Ball and the others. The ex-sapper had had his dream, and now he followed Ball, and countless other aces, into history. What the best of Germany's fighter force had failed to accomplish, an unknown marksman in a clogged trench on the Western Front had achieved with a single, lucky shot. And this humble soldier would never know for sure that it was his bullet which had done it.

Filled with these sad thoughts, the young Inglis flew away from the pillar of smoke, to take the grim news back to base.

Ball and Mannock are lustrous names in the history of military aviation, but no roll call of Allied air heroes in World War One is complete without mention of a third holder of the Victoria Cross—the Canadian ex-cavalryman Billy Bishop. Like "the Mad Major," Ontario-born

William Avery Bishop was fond of swooping low over the
trenches and exchanging greetings with the troops—and
on one occasion he went one better than that ; he and his
fighter plane actually took part in a bayonet charge across
no-man's-land !

This famous incident took place on Easter Monday, 1917,
in the opening phase of the Battle of Arras. British units
had been ordered "over the top," and were advancing
slowly across the pocked and boggy ground. Heavy and
accurate machine-gun fire from the German lines was
taking frightful toll, cutting great swathes in their ranks,
gradually bring them to a stop.

Bishop, circling overhead, saw the advance falter and
no-man's-land become heaped with dead and wounded.
But in one sector a determined formation of attackers had
got to within a few hundred yards of their objective.

Slicing down, he roared over the heads of his countrymen at about thirty feet, saw that they were being halted
and pinned down by the cross-fire from two machine-gun
posts. Banking, he turned, dropped still lower, flew
towards one of the posts, blasted it with long bursts. Then
for minutes on end he flew to and fro, ahead of the advancing Tommies, raking both enemy posts and a section
of the German trenches in between. At times, as he hauled
the plane round in a steep turn, his wingtips were only
inches from the ground.

So accurate was his shooting that the enemy gunners
were forced to break off. The British forces started forward again, bayonets high and glinting, moving steadily
through the drifting smoke in a solid, purposeful line.
Bishop circled overhead, waved encouragingly as they
broke into a stumbling charge, smashed through the
German front line.

And with the objective gained in this sector of the front, troops on either side rallied and continued their attacks. Thereafter Billy Bishop—who survived the war, to become an Air Marshal of the Royal Canadian Air Force, and an important influence in the development of air power—was also given the honoured title which Mannock had first inspired: " the Mad Major."

CHAPTER FIVE

THE WORST WEATHER IN THE WORLD

THE COCKPIT was awash. Cobham could no longer see ahead, for the force of the monsoon, hitting his goggles as from a high-pressure hose, completely blinded him. He tore them off and, snugging his head below the cockpit screen to avoid the full blast, squinted down over the side, seeking the vaguest shape of land below.

It was 9th September, 1926. Most of the following week the world was to hold its breath for news of Alan Cobham and his two companions, battling through savage storms in a tiny, single-engined seaplane. They had set out to prove that the worst weather in the world need not preclude a regular air service to Australia and back.

And this slight, urgent little Londoner with the trim moustache was on this occasion making no empty, glory-seeking gesture, but a sober investment of his life in the future of aviation. Now it seemed he was going to lose his great gamble.

Flying low over the sea, scanning a very inadequate map, Cobham had tried to zig-zag the little plane between the monsoon storms. But the moment he crossed the northern tip of Sumatra the full fury of the weather, sweeping unchecked across the Indian Ocean, closed round behind him and buried his plane in a terrible deluge.

In the cabin his two engineers—Ward, whom he had borrowed from the R.A.F. in Basra on the outward trip, and Capel, who had joined the venture in Australia—realised they were in gravest danger now. Obviously they couldn't go on. Ahead it was black as the inside of an ink bottle. Cobham turned the plane about, knowing their only hope was to find a gap in the weather behind. But there was no escape. The monsoon had closed completely around them.

Seasoned airmen and realists, they accepted their great gamble as lost and resigned themselves to death. Then suddenly there loomed ahead a dim shape—an island. Cobham strained his aching eyes to penetrate the swirling rain and saw that the water on the leeward side seemed comparatively calm. He knew this was their last chance.

The seaplane came lurching out of the sodden darkness and flopped on the heaving water. Almost before the cloud of spray settled, Ward and Capel were out on the floats. But when Cobham looked shorewards he saw no beach—only a mass of rocks. He would have to taxi out to sea, come in again, and search for a better spot.

Crossways over the big rollers the plane dipped and lurched. The two engineers, clinging precariously to the floats, were human counterweights that kept the machine more or less upright; the tops were blowing off the waves like snow off mountain peaks, and they breathed more water than air. Luckily the next bay showed a good beach. They struggled towards this haven.

Ward had to cast the sea anchor—a long canvas sleeve—before the engine could be cut. But the sudden drag all but hurled him into the sea and he had to let go. The sea anchor was lost.

Nothing for it now but to taxi in and beach the aircraft. Ward and Capel jumped waist deep into the rushing surf and, fighting every foot, tugged the floats up on the sand.

Then they lashed the plane to the nearest palm tree. Almost at once the storm started to slacken.

A lucky sun-shot, between tatters of cloud, fixed their position. They were right off the beaten sea track, on an uninhabited island about forty miles from the mainland of Siam. Rock and impenetrable jungle came tumbling right down to the sea. The only way out was to fly. And it became clear that they must leave soon, for Cobham noticed with alarm that the tide was coming in, lifting the seaplane and bumping its cardboard-thin floats up and down on the beach. The waterline showed that high tide would reach up to the wall of jungle, and that would be the end of their floats—perhaps of the plane.

Taking off out to sea would mean going downwind, and with those giant rollers running across their path they would never get into the air. So he decided to take off across the wind, riding the long way of the rollers.

It was a terrible business. They bumped and crashed over the water, slowly, slowly gathering speed. Twice, as the floats began to lift, a breaker reared and dealt them a mighty blow, swatting them back into the sea. But on the third try the machine staggered into the air, held its way for an agonising second or so, then, gaining a knot or two of air speed, gradually climbed away.

The visibility worsened steadily again as Cobham headed through the downpour for the main coastline. But they had not gone far when a whistling noise joined the engine note, and a bad vibration shuddered through the craft ; the rain had ruined the wooden propeller, and some of the fabric was coming off.

Cobham used all his skill and knowledge to nurse the maimed, failing seaplane along until he judged they were near the coast, then he throttled back and eased the stick forward. He could see only a few yards, but his judgment was perfect. They came down on to a heaving sea not far offshore from the tiny Siamese village of Tanoon. Once safely beached, the engineers busied themselves with repairs.

So ended 9th September, a worse day than most, though it marked neither the beginning nor by any means the end of a series of hair-raising incidents in the most epic survey flight yet attempted in the history of aviation.

What kind of man was this Cobham, who undertook such a flight ? What paths brought him to such high adventure ?

Alan Cobham was reared in the Camberwell district of London. As a boy he was impulsive, highly imaginative. After an uneventful journey in a pony trap, or a quiet day on the river, he could conjure up and invent the most hair-raising exploits which he would retell in convincing detail. Friends and members of the family feared that this vivid talent for " spinning a yarn " would lead him into trouble. But his mother defended him. She saw in those wild tales the outpourings of a mind desperate for excitement, a heart hungry for travel and action. And she could see in her son the beginnings of a fine quality which would balance this " romanticising "; he had a growing sense of responsibility, shown most clearly in his attitude towards his sister Vera—a girl with a weak heart.

The young Alan was Vera's loyal, self-appointed protector, eager for her happiness, constant in his companionship and always firm and shrewd in guarding her from the thousand petty dangers which lurk for the delicate child. With a quaint, almost fatherly sternness he would upbraid her for running while they were out in the park. And in the evenings those imagined adventures, told in gay boyish tones, let Vera share in a world she could never fully enjoy herself.

Perhaps the most memorable day in Alan's boyhood was when his mother took him to Crystal Palace to see a famous balloonist, Captain Spencer. Passionately the boy begged for a chance to go up in the balloon. Mrs. Cobham refused, told him : " You'll have more sense when you grow up—then you'll know it's better to stay on the ground."

When he left school, his first job was with a wholesale draper in the City of London. But a lad with the restless, adventure-craving heart of Alan Cobham could not take life sitting on an office stool. He tried farming—and gave that up too, because he found an open-air routine as monotonous as that of the City. Routine was the enemy—routine, and having to stay in one place.

One night he was returning home, deep in thoughts of how he might find the right job. He took the wrong bus and arrived in Brixton, on the other side of London. He asked his way from a stranger. They fell into conversation, and suddenly Alan found himself pouring out his troubles.

" They want chaps for the Royal Field Artillery—why not join up ? " the stranger suggested. " The Army has routine, all right—but you'll see a bit of the world, and perhaps some real excitement."

That was in early 1914. Cobham was at the front in France within a month of the outbreak of war. He saw plenty of action in the trenches, and in 1917, when a call went out for volunteers for the Royal Flying Corps, he was among the first to step forward. The R.F.C. training and experience convinced him that his destiny was in the air—always on the move, often in danger, never chained by routine. So after the war he went into civil aviation, and in 1922 was the first Englishman to cross the Channel in a light plane. Two years later he flew to Rangoon and back.

Newspapermen who interviewed him after the Rangoon flight saw him as a cheerful, superbly confident and relaxed young airman who seemed to find his work easy and enjoyable as any sport. But in fact Cobham took each and every task with great, almost grim earnestness—planning each detail, budgeting for the most unlikely eventuality. Just being a pilot wasn't enough—he made himself an expert in every branch of aviation, studying navigation, engineering, aerodynamics, aircraft design, radio communications and metereology. He kept abreast of research and development at home and abroad, studied scientific papers, and made long and frequent journeys to see demonstrations of new equipment.

With his growing knowledge of flying and the aircraft industry, he foresaw the day, not far off, when regular air services would link the continents, carrying urgent mail and perhaps even passengers on fixed schedules to the most distant parts of the globe. Other, older aviation experts scoffed at the idea—aeroplanes, unlike ships, were " fair weather " craft ; it would take many years to produce a machine powerful enough, and with the necessary equipment, endurance and structural strength, to make regular journeys over long distances all the year round, especially in tropical areas where storms of extreme violence developed suddenly.

Cobham, sure that skilled piloting and thorough planning could beat all the dangers, determined to prove it by flying to the other side of the world and back. If it could be done now, in an ordinary, frail plane not specially designed for the job, and without special equipment, then the leaders of Britain's aircraft industry surely would see the urgent need for larger, long-distance machines, and seize the chance to beat other nations in the new field of global air travel. It would be a gamble, but calculated—and with the future of British aviation at stake.

Such was the bold dream which now, in September, 1926, so nearly ended in disaster amid the killing combers off Siam.

In this epic flight to explore and map a new air route to Australia and back, Cobham had deliberately chosen to pit courage and wits, and a plane as vulnerable as a moth by to-day's standards, against the monsoon season at its furious height. And all to establish his conviction that the route could be flown throughout the year.

" My plan," he wrote subsequently, " was to make two jumps per day, keeping up anything from seven hundred to a thousand miles continually between dawn and sunset." He knew that in years to come, with the organisation which would follow his example, there would be better mapping and a system of wireless weather reporting which would enable pilots to miss or fly round the worst of the storms. But for him, the pioneer, skill and resolution were the only defences against the elements.

The odds which had faced Cobham when his aircraft rose from the Medway, at Rochester, on the last day of June that year elude the imaginative grasp of the modern air traveller. His machine—a De Havilland D.H. 50, registered " G-EFBO," powered by a single engine of a mere 383 horsepower—was overloaded by half a ton. It was fitted with seaplane floats, yet beyond a few trial " hops " squeezed in during his last busy week at home, Cobham had no experience of seaplane handling.

He had sketchy maps, no radio, hardly any weather prediction system to warn him of what lay ahead. The 13,000-mile route was dotted with volunteer helpers who, beyond instructions by cable and post, knew next to nothing about the requirements for the landing, mooring-up, servicing and taking-off of a seaplane. Some had never even seen one!

In his early planning, Cobham had allowed himself much too little time to organise the flight, and so had overworked himself to the point of exhaustion before starting. He admitted this later.

" I started off," he said, " on the verge of a nervous breakdown. I relied on the exhilaration of getting into the air and away to pull me round." It didn't. For the first week he flew in a state of collapse. More than once he dozed off at the controls. On his first few overnight stops he dreaded the dawn, when he must drag himself from his resting-place down to the seaplane's mooring.

Cobham's real troubles commenced when he ran into a desert dust storm between Baghdad and Basra. It was impenetrable. He nosed down until the plane was flying only a few feet above the reeds of a marsh, while he strove to make out a horizon by which he could hold the aircraft level.

Suddenly there was a violent explosion. He looked round and saw Elliott, the mechanic engaged for the round-trip, huddled in a corner clutching his side. Above the engine Elliott shouted: " Petrol pipe burst! I've been hit, Chief. Losing pots of blood!"

There was nothing for it but to make for Basra and hospital as fast as they could. The heat was furnace-fierce and Cobham landed perilously on a river littered with shipping. When Elliott had been rushed to hospital, Alan examined the plane and was sorely puzzled to find no damage to the fuel system.

The doctors cleared up the mystery: it wasn't a burst

petrol pipe which had hit Elliott—but a tribesman's bullet. He died the next night in hospital.

At that, Cobham almost lost heart. But cables from home urged him to go on, and the R.A.F. offered to lend him an engineer—a cheerful sergeant named Ward. This airman was to prove a jewel, for though the engine behaved gallantly, the way ahead was strewn with enough mishaps and make-do to keep a whole maintenance crew busy.

When they reached Allahabad, in India, they kept inquisitive native craft from colliding with them only by squirting the occupants with water, and narrowly missed hitting a railway bridge on take-off when the wind changed at the last minute. At Calcutta they had to take special care not to fall in the Hooghly River as they clambered about on the slippery, oil-streaked floats; the under-currents were so strong that they would never have come up again.

Then came the Burmese rains. Blue-black clouds advanced glowering out of the East to meet them. At times the deluge became a solid wall beyond which they could not see. Cobham kept low, twisting and turning to follow the rocky bays and inlets, close enough to be constantly terrified of crashing. He force-landed once, in a creek near Rangoon, frighteningly close behind a river steamer.

For the last leg of the outward trip, over the dreaded Timor Sea, Cobham laid a protractor upon an Admiralty map and took a bearing. He flew into the teeth of the South-East trade winds, which veered him first to port, then to starboard. He juggled with mental arithmetic and made rule-of-thumb corrections on his compass while flying fifty feet above the water. When the first long spit of land that was Australia rose over the horizon he climbed to have a look round. There, less than five miles away was his objective—Herne Bay. After 500 miles of dead-reckoning navigation in fickle winds, he had almost exactly hit his destination !

Cobham changed the floats for landing wheels at Darwin and flew across the continent to Sydney simply by following car tracks, mule trails and telegraph wires. The plains below, bathed in sharp, vibrating sunlight, seemed like one vast aerodrome. At Melbourne the largest crowd he had ever seen—more than 150,000—swarmed cheering on to the aerodrome and carried him off in triumph.

Despite all he had been through, Alan Cobham decided to make the return trip a record bid. With Capel, an extra engineer recruited in Melbourne to help Ward work on the plane during their brief stops, he took off and headed back, plunging almost immediately into foul weather.

The monsoon met him with avenging fury above Sumatra, and brought him down—first at the unknown island, then at Tanoon, then again at Victoria Point. And it maintained its onslaught with unrelenting savagery right into the heart of India. The diversions and delays cost him four days.

With all hope of a record now gone, the little weather-stained plane fought its way slowly up to Calcutta, where there was more bad news. The storm with which they had first collided, 1,600 miles to the South, had outstripped them and was now raging at Allahabad, their next stop 600 miles to the North. And yet they had to go on. For a tidal bore—a wall of water several feet high—was reported rolling up the Hooghly River. They knew it would wreck the machine at its moorings.

So the battle continued. . . . At Delhi the plane broke loose and drifted downcurrent towards a weir, while

Ward, astride a float, furiously plied a paddle. The paddle broke, and they all dived overboard, swimming and tugging at the floats. Somehow they managed to beach her.

Many other incidents and accidents tried their stamina, efficiency and resourcefulness before they neared the milder skies of Europe. Then all three started to scrub and polish the seaplane into cleanliness for the homecoming.

So at last the little blue-and-silver craft came up the Thames. " G-EFBO " circled Westminster, side-slipped daintily and came in, swaying a little, twenty feet over Westminster Bridge, to land on the river opposite the Houses of Parliament. There it glittered while Cobham walked up the Palace landing stairs in stained and rumpled dungarees—for he had jettisoned his " formals " with other non-essentials to offset the extra over-load of Capel. A vast crowd gave a thunderous welcome to the first man to fly to Australia and back.

Many a young London clerk was late back from lunch that day. No doubt some of them, like Cobham, had thought of revolt from a City stool. In this man in dungarees they saw not only a great aviator, but an individual who had rebelled against routine, sought and found adventure. How many clerks and schoolboys who watched round-eyed the return of Cobham, the trailblazer, later followed him across the same skies—in peace and in war? And how many others, thrilled by his story, were encouraged to find careers in technical branches of aviation? The full extent of this airman's personal contribution to British air power can never be known in exact terms.

That Australian trip brought him the Britannia Trophy and a knighthood. Cobham, in his superb gamble, had challenged and defied the worst weather in the world;

he had proved that a British plane could outwit nature in her angriest moods; he had shown that flying was no " fair-weather sport," and he had set pilots practising a new art—" blind flying," by the new cockpit instruments.

Sir Alan went on to other ventures—a flying-boat expedition round the continent of Africa; a memorable trip to Capetown, and later air displays with the famous " Cobham's Air Circus." Everything he did served to popularise flying, to excite and inspire youngsters.

His weather-warring wings widened the world for coming generations. The boy with the untameable imagination, who hated routine, became one of the greatest trail-blazers in the history of flying; one of the founders of the proud tradition which many years later sustained and emboldened that small, hard-pressed band of pilots known as The Few in their vital defence of Britain against vastly superior forces.

CHAPTER SIX

AMERICA'S LOYAL REBEL

WHEN JAPANESE planes splintered out of the clouds over
Pearl Harbour on 7th December, 1941, and at a single, swift
blow destroyed many of America's most powerful warships
and the U.S. Navy's main Pacific base, the defending
commanders reported to Washington : " We were taken
completely by surprise—we got no warning of any
kind."

But many American newspapers and radio newscasters
grimly reminded the shocked nation that the defence
chiefs had been warned of this attack *fully eighteen years
before*—indeed, the Japanese methods had been described
in accurate detail. And the prophet who had spotted the
weaknesses in the defence systems of Hawaii and the
Philippines, and shown how Japan could deliver a crushing
assault in this area unless air preparedness was increased,
had been fiercely reprimanded by the General Staff, sneered
at by the politicians, finally disgraced and deprived of his
career—Brigadier-General William Mitchell, Assistant
Chief of Military Aviation, U.S. Army.

Mitchell had died in 1936, of a heart disease aggravated
by overwork, disregard of medical advice, prolonged
strain, frustration and the most bitter disappointment.
Court-martialled and forced to resign from the service as
a result of his outspoken criticisms and accusations, he
had been making his living by breeding and training horses

in Milwaukee. At his funeral there was not even a military escort—but despite foul weather a number of army pilots in that part of the country took off unofficially and flew low over the cemetery, dipping their wings in last salute to the man that they, as military airmen, regarded as their brilliant champion.

Now, as Mitchell's forecasts became awesome reality and an ill-prepared America was thrown into war, at last his genius and patriotism were appreciated by all his countrymen. In January, 1942, the Senate voted to restore him posthumously to the Army with full rank. And four long, hard years later—on 25th July, 1946—a Congress that had victory in its grasp recognised the part that the dead Mitchell had played in the struggle, and authorised the striking of a special medal which would honour him for his pioneer work in aviation.

Billy Mitchell was not a dashing war pilot, a record-breaker or a stunt-man. His toughest battles were fought on the ground—on lecture platforms, in conference rooms, in government offices and in the columns of newspapers and magazines. Yet his is a story of the highest human courage and great sacrifice—qualities which place him prominently in the ranks of the world's unforgettable air heroes. The son of a Milwaukee farmer who had risen to distinction as a United States senator, Mitchell from his boyhood lived in a progressive, vital atmosphere. His grandfather, Alexander Mitchell, had come to America from Scotland in 1839, and made important contributions to the development of the West, building railroads, setting up trading companies and banks. Scots hardiness, and the pioneer spirit, dominated the family life.

Entering the Army in 1898 as a private soldier, he

earned rapid promotion and served in the Spanish-American War and the Philippine Insurrection. A meeting with Orville Wright in 1908 deeply impressed Captain Mitchell. With the outbreak of World War One he turned his energies and experience to aviation, and became commander of the air forces, American Expeditionary Forces, in the battles over France in 1917-18.

By 1921, Brigadier-General Mitchell was in his early forties and already had had a warning, from a doctor consulted in private, that his heart was strained and he should rest. But the slightly-built, energetic, volatile officer was engrossed in a task which he believed was vitally important to his country's security—and to complete this work he must continue to fly, leading his young pilots in long and difficult training exercises, day after day. Somehow, by pleading pressure of duties, he managed to avoid the regular, routine medical examinations by Army physicians.

Mitchell's aim was to prove to America's statesmen and military leaders that in any future war they would have to fight not just with the Army and the Navy, but also with a third, equally important service which should be largely independent of the other two—the air force. It wasn't good enough just to have a few squadrons working with the Army, and a few more serving the Fleet—he wanted Washington to start thinking in terms of what he called " air power," and to provide money for the building of a large, quite separate organisation equipped with modern fighters and bombers.

An expert on modern bombing techniques, he had long sought a chance to demonstrate the shattering effects of a properly planned, competently executed raid. He wrote a sensational book, *Our Air Force*, and enraged Navy

brass-hats by stating that ships without air support were
" easy meat " for bombers, that even the biggest of them
could be sunk from a range of two or three thousand feet.
" Ridiculous ! " roared the admirals. Provoked into
loud mockery, they could not refuse his challenge—to let
him put his theory to actual test, using captured German
warships as his targets. Josephus Daniels, secretary of
the Navy, offered to " stand bareheaded at the wheel of
any battleship Mitchell proposes to bomb." . . . but
nobody took him up on it.

After much procrastination, the tests at last were fixed
to begin on 20th June. Mitchell and his crack crews trained
with unsparing concentration ; they knew their aircraft
and equipment were old and none too reliable, and that
their own skill and determination would be vital to success.
The young flyers believed, too, that if they failed their
leader's career would be damaged—he would be discredited,
regarded as a braggardly eccentric.

The morning dawned still and misty over Chesapeake
Bay. As the mist lifted, the early sun glinted on a vast
array of fighting ships—dreadnoughts, destroyers, mine-
sweepers. And in the centre of the bay, anchored at some
distance from all the other vessels, rode the former German
submarine U-117, the target.

On the decks of the biggest warships were Congressmen,
members of the Cabinet, Army and Navy brass-hats,
newspaper correspondents and photographers, emissaries
and military attachés from several foreign countries and
their wives and relatives. The atmosphere was festive,
the conversation witty—they were all going to have an
entertaining time at the expense of this boastful idiot
Mitchell.

The formation of frail and elderly planes droned out of

the landward haze. They dropped twelve small bombs on the U-117. The submarine rolled on her side, sank swiftly beneath the calm water. The bombers resumed formation, turned for home. The entire operation, from the moment the planes were sighted to the disappearance of the U-boat's conning tower, had taken exactly sixteen minutes.

The newspapermen and some of the more progressive Army chiefs were obviously impressed, but the Navy brass-hats and most of the politicians declared that nothing had been proved—naval gunfire could have sunk the U-117 in half the time; the bombers had not had to fly through A.A. fire, or any other opposition, and the target had been perfectly stationary. Mitchell made no reply to these jeers, for this was just the beginning of the long and carefully planned series of tests which he had fought so hard to have agreed by the Navy and Washington.

The next test, on 29th June, was out of his hands any-way—an entirely Navy affair. An old American battleship, kept in motion by remote radio control, was attacked by twenty-five Navy planes. They dropped eighty bombs, made only two hits. The Navy brass-hats said this showed it was next-to-impossible to hit a moving vessel from an aircraft. General Mitchell said it showed only that the Navy pilots were poor marksmen.

Then 13th July saw him personally lead the attack again —this time against the former German destroyer, G-102. First he sent in twelve fighters. They screamed down on the ship, straffed her decks with their machine-guns. Then the bombers struck, with deadly accuracy. The destroyer was gone in less than twenty minutes.

The excuses from the brass-hats this time sounded weak and captious—the destroyer had been very old, unsea-

worthy, about to sink of her own volition, almost. . . .
She was only lightly armoured, there had been no anti-
aircraft fire. . . . To Mitchell and his few supporters it was
becoming sickeningly obvious that the Navy's top men
weren't really interested in getting at the truth, that their
only aim was to preserve the Navy's reputation for
" invulnerability " and to stop defence funds, which might
be used to build more ships, being allocated to aircraft
development. They were putting loyalty to their own service before loyalty to their country.

On 19th July, the target was the big, ex-German light
cruiser *Frankfurt*, which had heavy armour and first class
watertight compartmentation. So confident was the Navy
that the bombers would fail that they had arranged to sink
her by gunfire after the attempt . . .

It was agreed that Mitchell would attack first with 300-
pound bombs, then with 600-pounders. Late in the
morning, after the first strike, naval umpires inspected the
damage on board the target-ship and reported with obvious
delight that the watertight bulkheads were holding.

In the afternoon the bomb-aimers, showing the greatest
skill and coolness, took care to drop several of the larger
missiles not on the *Frankfurt*, but close alongside. The
first explosion lifted the great vessel right out of the water.
As the other bombs rained down she began to settle deeper,
deeper. . . . Thirty-two minutes after the first 600-pounder
had fallen, she had vanished beneath the waves. The sledge-
hammer blows from the explosions close around her hull
had smashed in her plates, twisted and ruptured her watertight bulkheads.

Now the brass-hats kept an alarmed, hostile silence.
The test programme had one final stage to go, an attack
on the huge German battleship *Ostfriesland*—if Mitchell

failed on that, then everything he had done so far could be dismissed, forgotten.

On 20th July, the weather joined the opposition—thick, low clouds and a high, gusty wind. The air crews had been training frantically for this last and biggest trial. Mitchell had been robbing himself of sleep, going without meals; he was haggard with strain—and very probably secretly in pain from his heart ailment. As the crews stood by their loaded planes, waiting for the Navy to signal " target and observers ready, take-off," he told them ; " This is going to be a tough nut to crack, boys, but we'll do it. Then we can all have a bit of a rest."

But the signal to take-off didn't come. The tired leader's patience snapped, he clambered into a reconnaissance machine and headed out to the target area to find out what was wrong. To his surprise and fury, he saw the entire Fleet preparing to sail away from the target—apparently taking it for granted that the bombers would be useless in the windy, cloudy conditions ! Resolutely he signalled that his force was ready to attack. The Fleet stayed where it was.

When Mitchell got back over the target area leading his formation, frantic signals from the ships ordered them to keep away from the target, hover and await further direction. An inspection party was on board the *Ostfriesland*. The bombers had to circle for very nearly an hour, with the weather worsening steadily, before they got the "all clear."

As they started to make their bombing runs, signals from the shore warned them that a full-blown storm was on the way. And even as they drew near the target mounting gusts of wind caught them, tossed them violently, and driving sheets of rain partially obscured the scene below

"Unload," the Navy umpires signalled impatiently. "Observers at readiness."

Bad weather they could take, but a fierce squall like this made it impossible to hold the planes steady, to line up properly on the target. Yet they couldn't withdraw, they had to go through with it now.

In the circumstances it was a marvel that they hit the ship at all. The superstructure was severely damaged. There was no hope of sinking her.

That night jubilant Navy brass-hats gave interviews to pressmen, declaring that all the bomber planes in the world, manned by the most skilled crews, couldn't sink one sea-worthy battleship. Mitchell was a crank, a wild dreamer, a career-man, seeking publicity and personal glory at the expense of the people's confidence in the Fleet. And next morning the headlines told the nation: "FLYERS FAIL TO SINK BATTLESHIP. . . . NOTHING TO FEAR FROM THE AIR, SAY NAVY CHIEFS. . . . BILLY MITCHELL'S BOMBERS FLOP. . . ."

But, according to the test agreement, Mitchell had the right to try once more. This time conditions were in his favour—a glassy sea, very little cloud. Flying his own small, personal plane, the *Osprey*, he led eight Martins to the attack. From 2,000 feet the first plane scored a direct hit on the foredeck. At once, quite inexplicably, the Navy's control ship signalled: "Cease firing!" But the bombers, having started their attack, could not be withdrawn instantly. Before they broke off, four more bombs had been dropped—scoring two more direct hits. "Cease firing, cease firing!" came the frantic signal from below. Mitchell, smouldering with inner rage, took his planes back to base.

His strong protests brought no explanation of why he had been ordered to break off. He demanded the right to resume, and this was reluctantly agreed—but only three of his biggest bombs, the 2,000-pounders, were to be dropped.

Mitchell was shocked, sickened—he had a written agreement with the Navy which said that the flyers would be allowed to make two direct hits with these giant missiles, and to that end could drop as many as were necessary. But now, after what had happened to the *Frankfurt*, the Navy knew that near-hits, exploding in the water close around a vessel, could deal deadly blows, too. So now they were trying to restrict what was supposed to be a competent air strike on a capital ship to just three of the big bombs, hits or misses. . . .

The General made a vital and fateful decision. Though he knew he certainly was placing his entire career in jeopardy, and that he had powerful enemies who would seize any excuse to smash him, he decided to ignore this new order and abide by the written agreement. Flying was his life's work, his livelihood—but he put his country first.

Shortly after noon he took off again, leading six Martins and one British-built Handley Page out on their last, decisive flight of the test programme. The very first 2,000-pounder struck the port bow, glanced off into the water. In his own description Mitchell said : " Up came a spout of water—higher than any missile made by man had ever produced. The bomb must have lifted 60 million pounds of water, or 27,000 tons, which was more than the total tonnage of the battleship. And as it settled, about a half of this fell on the *Ostfriesland's* decks, from an average height of several hundred feet."

But to the observers on the decks of ships moored within sight of the target, the explosion seemed to have no effect.

When the curtain of spray had gone, the *Ostfriesland* had not stirred.

Two more big bombs. With the third, the dreadnought appeared to lift slightly, then settle back evenly. The fourth and fifth entered the water close alongside, and her nose for an instant rose, clear of the sea, then fell back. The Navy began sending angry signals—" Cease firing ! Three heavies maximum. . . ." But Mitchell ignored this.

A watching Admiral grinned broadly, told his officers, " Let them carry on—look at the target, she's undamaged ! All they're managing to do is wash down her decks. This is the best possible proof that a battleship just can't be sunk from the air ! " But even as he spoke a young Lieutenant at his elbow gave a gasp, handed him binoculars. The Admiral focused the glasses on the target, and then slowly lowered them from a face that was going the colour of lead. The binoculars weren't necessary—now everybody in the observation ships could see very clearly the proud *Ostfriesland's* bows rising slowly, majestically, high in the air, revealing great, gaping wounds below her waterline. She slid backward, gently, smoothly.

Just twenty-one-and-a-half minutes after the release of the first 2,000-pounder, the " unsinkable " battleship had vanished, on her way to the bottom.

In the cockpit of the little *Osprey*, Mitchell looked down on the huge, widening white stain that marked the *Ostfriesland's* grave. His muscles throbbed, his eyes prickled from want of sleep, but he could not resist diving, sweeping low over the spot, and then at mast-height across the decks of the observation ships, waggling his wings in triumph.

Back at base, he was hauled from the cockpit amid deafening cheers. Ground crews, pilots, newspapermen and even a few politicians wanted to congratulate him, pledge their support. It seemed that at last he had won a complete victory, that his ideas must be acclaimed and accepted by every honest, logical statesman and military chief, and that the birth of a strong, independent air force would be regarded as more important than the completion of the Navy's ambitious three-year capital ship programme.

But the most bitter disappointment of all—the blow which, some say, almost broke Mitchell's already over-strained heart—came a few weeks later when it became obvious that Washington was going to take no definite action as a result of the tests. The Navy brass-hats sneeringly dismissed Mitchell's achievements as " a fluke—sheer luck." Secretary of War, John Weeks, was alleged to have declared sourly that he wasn't going to be stampeded " by that circus performer." And the eagerly awaited report on the tests, published by the Joint Board of the U.S. Army and Navy, and signed by Chief of Staff General Pershing, concluded : " The battleship is still the backbone of the Fleet, and will so remain as long as the safe navigation of the sea for purposes of trade or transportation is vital to success in war." As a result, the Navy's capital ship programme went ahead, and the funds allocated for aviation development were *reduced*.

The sad, the alarming part of it was that other nations had been deeply impressed by Mitchell's demonstrations. Many, including Japan—who had had an air observer at the tests—launched large-scale programmes to build up air power. This troubled the patriotic airman much more than his own ill health, and the fact that the War Department now decided to promote another officer, over his head, as commander of the Air Service—leaving him as Assistant Chief.

Ordered to rest, for a while he occupied himself with

other projects, among them a technique for refuelling aircraft in flight, which he evolved in partnership with the great aviation pioneer and designer Alexander de Seversky. In 1923 he toured Hawaii, Japan and the Philippines. Shocked by the poor state of the defences in the Pacific, sickened by the petty jealousies between Army and Navy units, and thoroughly alarmed by Japan's growing strength and progressive attitude to military flying, he compiled a detailed, fiercely critical report for Washington. In this, he placed himself in the boots of a Japanese commander and set out a plan for a surprise attack on American bases in the Pacific. (Eighteen years later, the attack took place, almost exactly as he described it.)

Severely reprimanded as " an outrageous war-monger, seeking to make trouble between friendly neighbours ", he was called home to face a Congressional inquiry. He accused high-ranking representatives of both the Army and the Navy of " deliberately falsifying reports with intent to deceive the country," and kept hammering home the warning that in Japan he had found sixteen huge aircraft factories, most of them working round-the-clock, while here in the U.S. there wasn't one plane manufacturer working anywhere near capacity. He was reduced to his permanent rank of Colonel, and posted to a remote training camp in Texas, where his adversaries thought he would be " unable to make trouble."

But nobody could stop him taking occasional, unofficial trips, to visit friends on important bases. On one of these visits he inspected the Navy's great airship, the *Shenandoah*. His technical knowledge and his airman's eye told him at once the dirigible was unsafe—and he said so, loudly and sharply. But nothing was done. Not long afterwards—despite the protests of the airship's commander,

Lieutenant-Commander Zachary Landsdowne—she was ordered to make a flying tour of state fairs in the Mid-West. She ran into a storm on 3rd September, 1925, broke apart and crashed. Of her 42-man crew, fourteen perished.

Mitchell was filled with anger and sorrow—he saw the *Shenandoah* disaster as only one example of the way that lives were being thrown away, and the country's security jeopardised, by mismanagement of air defences. He came to yet another vital decision; in a last desperate effort to bring reforms, he would move into the open, tell the American people the plain truth as he saw it. He knew that this would be regarded as a gross breach of loyalty on the part of an officer—especially an officer of his rank and experience—and that whatever happened he would be court-martialled. But with Billy Mitchell, it was always the nation first, and personal problems were a secondary consideration.

He called a press conference, told the tense reporters: " These accidents . . . are the result of the incompetence, the criminal negligence, the almost treasonable administration of our national defence by the Navy and War Departments.

" The Army and Navy," he said, " have formed a sort of union to perpetuate their own existence, largely irrespective of public welfare, and acting as ' an illegal combination in the restraint of trade. . . .' Not one heavy bomb has been dropped by our Air Service in target practice in two years. . . . Our pilots know they are going to be killed if they stay in the service, because of the old flaming coffins we are still flying. . . .

" Gentlemen, we would not be keeping our trust with our departed comrades were we longer to conceal the facts."

These words, under huge headlines, stunned the country. From Washington the brass-hats screeched "Maniac! Traitor!" Mitchell was "a madman trying to stampede the people into panic." He was "scaring ordinary, loyal Americans with his horror stories—his imaginary capture of the Philippines and Hawaii by Japan, a peace-loving friend." And then, within a few days, there were more huge headlines : " Court-Martial for Colonel Mitchell."

The charge was violation of the 96th Article of War which stated with great vagueness : " All conduct of a nature liable to bring discredit upon the military service shall be punished at the discretion of the court." And the judges for the trial included no air officer—in fact, it was doubtful if any of them had ever been up in a plane.

In his defence, trying to prove that his accusations were wholly justified, Mitchell presented facts and figures. For instance, he said, the War Department, in computing U.S. air strength, spoke of a total of 1,820 aircraft. But only 69 of these machines could be called " modern," and of those sixty were being used for training purposes—" *leaving only nine planes available for the air defence of the United States.*"

Many other leading pilots gave evidence for the defence —notably the renowned " ace " Eddie Rickenbacker, and the future General " Hap " Arnold. During the exacting three weeks of the trial, inevitably Mitchell's heart condition worsened, but he ignored his doctors' advice to ask the court for an adjournment so that he could rest and have treatment.

The court found him guilty—apparently indifferent to the disquieting facts and figures, concerned only with the embarrassment he had caused service chiefs, an embarrassment which the bench interpreted as " bringing discredit upon the military service." The verdict was not unanimous : Major General Douglas MacArthur, destined to be conqueror of Japan years later, was one of the few judges who found him innocent. They did not dismiss him from the Army—because if he became a civilian, no longer subject to military laws, he could criticise as much as he pleased and cause a great deal more " embarrassment." The sentence was highly unusual; five years suspension, with loss of rank and pay.

But Mitchell would not be muzzled. He immediately resigned from the Army, and in doing so he said : "I look back with pride and satisfaction that I have done everything I could for my country . . . I shall always be at hand, in case of war or emergency, whenever I am needed."

He was needed almost at once—by those fair-minded, progressive Americans (and they were many now, in all parts of the Union and in all walks of life) who, jolted fully awake by the revelations of the trial, launched a series of campaigns calling for a study of the true conditions of America's national defence, and for the development of aviation to create a third element in that defence—" air power." Despite the verdict, despite his public disgrace, Mitchell at last had won a great victory ; and now—as a civilian—he fought fiercely and tirelessly at the head of this new and growing force of opinion, travelling the country, lecturing, writing articles, interviewing, seeking out young and far-sighted politicians, journalists and airmen. At the same time he managed to write a moving and impressive book, *Skyways*.

From all this feverish activity he earned little money. He invested his savings in horse-breeding and training—a hobby, begun in his first years as a private solider, which he hoped now would provide his family with security. In February, 1936, his over-strained heart collapsed. The doctors couldn't save him, he had too long disregarded their advice.

If ever a man sacrificed himself for his country, it was Billy Mitchell. And the passing of a few years—the remorseless tread of history—was to prove him right in almost all of his predictions, theories and policies. The brass-hats who opposed and disgraced him to-day are forgotten names, but Mitchell lives on, an American hero.

The creation of a separate U.S. Air Force, the building of immense air power—these things which were his dearest dreams have come to pass. The court-martial verdict has been laid aside, his country has admitted its tragic error and its everlasting debt to him. It is recognised that if Mitchell had not shown the way, fearlessly and expertly demonstrated the weaknesses in defence and thereby forced the next generation of air officers and administrators to see the desperate need for aviation reform and development, then after Pearl Harbour the United States might have found it impossible to gather her strength and swing quickly into all-out production of the right sort of aircraft, and the right sort of men to fly and command them.

Of all the honours which his repentant country showered on him years after he was gone, probably the pioneer of aerial bombing would have liked best the fact that the type of aircraft used for America's first raid on the Japanese mainland was known as the Mitchell bomber. This famous operation, in April, 1942, was commanded by another great fighter for air power, Colonel Jimmy Doolittle, and it was made possible by the whole-hearted, friendly co-operation of the U.S. Navy. For the Fleet carried Doolittle's force across a vast expanse of hostile ocean to within 600 miles of the target on board one of its biggest carriers, the *Hornet*.

And as the twin-engined Mitchells took off and headed west, officers on the carrier and the escort vessels solemnly saluted. This was another age, another Navy—and those officers who watched the bombers go had the deepest respect for the hitting-power of the modern war-plane, and for the skill and courage of the flyers. Working together on the best of terms, flyers and sailors were delivering a tremendous surprise blow to their country's vicious enemy; and other, even bigger blows would follow.

This mutual respect, and this mutual strength, were exactly what Billy Mitchell had fought, and given his all for, long years before.

CHAPTER SEVEN

LAST HOP TO HOWLAND

GEORGE PUTNAM PALMER, the New York publisher, looked into the wide grey eyes of the slender young woman who sat, relaxed and yet grave, facing him across his office desk. " Why do you want this job ? " he asked.

" Because I believe a person must try to do difficult, and especially dangerous things—that's the only way to find out the true extent of one's capabilities. If we stop trying, we stop developing, and we never get to know ourselves properly . . . I also believe that nowadays women must try to do things as men have been trying for hundreds of years."

She said all this evenly, unemotionally, with the clearest kind of sincerity. Putnam knew his problem was solved —the problem of finding an intelligent, level-headed, hardy yet attractive American girl willing to accompany his airmen friends, Lou Gordon and Wilmer Stultz, on their proposed Atlantic flight.

In 1928, crossing the Atlantic by plane was still an immensely hazardous business, a supreme test of man and machine. It had been done only ten times, and never by a woman. Gordon and Stultz had hit on the idea of taking along a girl as passenger, because they wanted an American woman to be the first across, and because they believed that such an achievement by " a mere female " would greatly increase the public's confidence in the future of air travel. They had asked George Putnam to find the right girl, for not only was he a fine judge of character, but a man who well knew the qualities needed for such an adventure, having twice led expeditions into the Arctic.

Now, after countless interviews, the right girl turned out to be Miss Amelia Earhart, teacher and social worker. Putnam had known her for some time, and remembering her strong interest in aviation, her self-confidence and her love of travel, after weeks of fruitless searching had sent her a message asking if she was interested in the idea. For answer, she had come straight to his office, full of restrained excitement.

He studied her now, as she read a summary of the primary flight plan. A long, slack girl with tameless, tawny hair and a quick, eager voice. Not pretty—but her boyish, freckled, very American face, those frank grey eyes, and the sudden, warm way she had of smiling added up to an attractive, completely unaffected personality. Not young, either—yet her boyishness, and her earnestness, made it hard to believe she was thirty. Born in Atchison, Kansas, she had first flown with the young and famous " barnstormer " Frank Hawks, then learned to pilot herself. But flying was expensive ; she had been unable to keep it up.

" You do understand the many risks involved ? "

She raised her head and gave him a steady, faintly puzzled look.

" Of course. If there were no danger, it wouldn't interest me. To achieve something, there *must* be risks."

Putnam smiled, nodded, lifted his telephone to arrange a meeting with Gordon and Stultz.

And so, a few weeks later, Amelia became the first woman to fly the Atlantic Ocean. Throughout the long, difficult and exhausting flight she remained alert and excited, intensely interested in everything the pilots did, tirelessly watching the instruments and, now and then when she was sure she wouldn't be distracting or fatiguing them, asking questions which showed she had a natural understanding of technicalities and a sound grasp of the principles of flight. And when it was all over she announced: " I'm going to do this again—on my own."

By writing and lecturing about her trip she acquired a little capital. From then on aeroplanes became her sole obsession. George Putnam helped her in every way he could to become a top-class pilot, but tried just as hard to discourage the wild notion of the hazardous solo crossing. Again and again he got her to postpone preparations for the attempt, using any convenient pretext—he would tell her that a new type of machine, or engine, was about to be produced which would give her a much better chance; or some branch of her flying was weak, she must spend a few more weeks correcting the fault. . . .

Putnam not only admired this extraordinary girl, he had gained a deep affection for her, and was determined not to let her risk her life. But Amelia—fiercely self-reliant, and with a passionate sense of freedom—would not allow even this greatly valued friendship to turn her from the target she had set herself. In flying she had found a new life, a new and more powerful self. She was confident she could beat the Atlantic, single-handed—and after that, perhaps other oceans.

In 1931, with several important cross-country flights behind her, she told Putnam: " I'm ready now. Please don't try to talk me out of it again. I won't hear of any more delay."

" All right, Amelia," he sighed. " But I have one more thing to ask before you go." And he asked her to become his wife.

Amelia did not give him an immediate answer. To her, marriage was now a danger, a threat to the great plans she had made; she wanted time to think. As a wife, would she be able to keep on flying as often as she liked, wherever she liked? Or would the responsibilities of a home gradually turn her into just another captive of the kitchen, dreaming sadly over the dirty dishes? And would it be fair to George, who had his own brilliant career, if she kept on with an occupation that demanded fullest attention, took her far from home, and involved constant tension and dangers?

She knew George Putnam was the only man for her, but she was determined that if they married it would have to be on the basis of a clear understanding; he must never try to stop her flying. Never.

Putnam gave this pledge, for he realised now that nothing could keep her on the ground, and he had come to respect her resolution and superb concentration. On their wedding day, a few hours before the ceremony, she handed him a remarkable letter, reminding him of their pact:

Dear G.P.,

There are some things which should be written before we are married. . . . You must know again my reluctance, my feeling that I shatter thereby chances in work which means so much to me. . . . I may have to keep some place where I can go to be myself now and then, for I cannot guarantee to endure at all times the confinements of even an attractive cage. . . .

It was fortunate that Putnam—the former Arctic explorer—understood the restless spirit in Amelia, the honesty and the passion for independence which had moved her to write such words on her wedding day.

The following year—1932—she flew the Atlantic alone. In a crimson Lockheed monoplane, she won for herself the title "First lady of U.S. Aviation" and set up a new record, thirteen-and-a-half hours. A complicated, rough flight through tricky, swirling winds and thickets of foul weather. Flames and fumes from a broken weld in an exhaust pipe leaked into the cockpit. The altimeter and the petrol gauge failed. Only a tough and workmanlike pilot, and an able navigator, could have battled successfully through the murk and the long, lonely, lurching hours.

Her name and her image flashed around the world. Millions came to know the freckled face with the tomboyish grin, under the short, rumpled hair. In the years that followed she remained headline news, making one important flight after another, the world's most famous and hardest-working air-woman.

In 1935, she made the first solo crossing of the Pacific, from Hawaii to California, in eighteen hours and sixteen minutes. She took deep interest in new types of machines—notably the autogyro, forerunner of the helicopter, which she flew frequently—and wrote and lectured brilliantly on every aspect of flying. And she never tired of encouraging young women who wanted to take to the air, often tutoring them herself, and—it was rumoured—sometimes paying their expenses out of her own pocket.

Those who worked with her in those crowded years, when she seemed to be trying to move events faster than they would in normal circumstances, when her tireless endeavours kept knocking cracks in the barriers to world-wide air travel, wondered at her apparent casualness which, combined with her ever-youthful smile, at times made her appear flippant, careless perhaps. It was almost as if she treated this work as an absorbing game, that she did not fully realise the tremendous chances she was taking—that she never thought of herself being destroyed, as so many others had been, by clutching, cleaving metal or hissing flames.

But the flippancy was only a pose. This perky spirit the newspapers dubbed " everybody's kid sister " knew the dangers, and knew fear too, and was not careless in the smallest respect. Only her husband and a few close friends knew that her light-heartedness was tempered by the greatest thoroughness in her labours, an unfailing scrupulosity in preparing for each new venture and, very occasionally, by a strange streak of melancholy.

She knew she was working all the time now very close to the limits of reliability of her equipment, and of her own stamina and skill, yet unless she was close to the limits the enterprise held no thrill for her, and with each fresh achievement the limits seemed to be extended. She was caught up in a fascinating race. She had to keep on striving, improving—she never forgot that she'd been late starting, and felt she had to make up for the lost years before she took to the air. Despite the constant, inner strain it all agreed with her; adventure was her nature.

To begin with, after each new success Putnam hoped she would give up flying, of her own free will. But in time he came to realise that the story must run on for many more chapters—neither of them could stop the pages turning now, or close the book. Amelia had chosen to be what she was, and had proved herself outstanding; it would be a long time before she would be ready to return to being just ordinary. And he had given his promise never to interfere.

Naturally he took great pride in her prowess, but he never ceased to dread losing her. He could never quite master this sort of life, never live it with the nerves alone, with his mind and emotions in cold storage. Each time he found himself sitting through endless hours in some airfield control tower, waiting for news of her, watching the clock's hands creep nearer to the limit of her aircraft's endurance, listening to weather reports and newspapermen weighing her chances, speculating on where and how she could have gone down, and chainsmoking and drinking great mugs of coffee all through the night—each time he went through that, he swore to himself it would be the last time. She'd done enough, promise or no promise he was going to take her home where a wife belonged, and keep her home, and for all the other nights she would be sitting by him, safe in the lamplight. . . .

But always, when at last the brave note of her engine reached his straining ears . . . when her wheels rested once more on solid ground and she clambered out of the machine wearing an old flying jacket with a fur collar, with her hair tousled, her eyes glazed and her features blurred with fatigue . . . when the crowds cheered and the cameras flashed, when she raised a weary arm to wave and that old, quick smile lifted the tired lines of her face—always the relief and the admiration for this extraordinary woman welled up so strong in him as he hurried to greet her that he forgot the vows he'd made in his hours of anxiety.

In 1937, in recognition of her great services to aviation, she was presented with a brand new, twin-engined Lockheed plane, the *Electra*, packed with so many up-to-date devices that the press named it "Earhart's flying laboratory." After thorough trials, having familiarised herself with the operation and capabilities of every piece of equipment on board, she told her husband : " This is the plane I'm going to fly round the world."

This round-the-world flight was a dream Amelia had cherished ever since her first success, the solo crossing of the Atlantic. Over all the busy years since then it had kept her going through difficulties, disappointments and occasional fits of depression. Everything up till now had been merely training, a rehearsal for the real test.

Though she didn't admit it, Amelia must have known that at last her staying power was beginning to go. She was 39—she must face the fact that soon her concentration and her judgment would lose their diamond-precision, she would tire more easily. It was now or never.

Deeply grateful to the wonderful husband who had made her career possible, who had been her wise and generous counsellor through it all, and who had kept his word never to try to curtail her flying, she told him with a wistfulness that was rare in her : " I've a feeling that there's just about one good flight left in my system, and I hope this is it. Anyway darling, after this I'm giving up major long-distance trips—I'll be coming home to be just plain Mrs. George Putnam, the publisher's wife."

She took off from Oakland, California, on a fine summer's day. With her was one of the country's most experienced and distinguished aerial navigators, Fred Noonan, who had pioneered the long and difficult San Francisco-to-Manila route for Pan American Airways, and guided that company's great *China Clipper* aircraft safely through many other important survey flights.

Forecasts on the weather ahead were good, but both these seasoned flyers knew how swiftly conditions could change, and their calculations left a margin for squalls, veering winds, and having to climb over thunder-clouds.

Yet surprisingly, there were no sudden changes, everything went smoothly all the way across the American continent to Florida . . . from Florida to Brazil . . . on the long hop across to Africa, and eastward on across baking deserts, jungles, mountains and sparkling seas to India. The skies smiled, *Electra* functioned perfectly.

It was at Lae, in New Guinea, with the flight almost finished, that they ran into trouble. The sky above the tiny air-strip, carved out of primeval jungle, grew black with storm-clouds, boomed with thunder, blazed with livid scars of lightning. Rain hissed down, in huge drops that stabbed deep into the sandy ground, and kept them prisoners for almost three days.

While she waited, Amelia re-checked her flight plans for the final lap. Her next stop was Howland Island, a fragment of coral rock in the middle of the vast Pacific, 2,556 miles away. It was the longest hop she had ever attempted, and to make room for the extra fuel and oil it required she had arranged to lighten the plane by discarding everything but essential equipment and emergency gear—drinking water, first-aid box, iron rations, a two-man rubber dinghy, flares, lifebelts, a Very pistol and signalling lamps. Even so *Electra* would be laden to capacity, and she knew the take-off from this short strip, with the jungle trees reaching up at one end and a cliff falling sheer to the sea at the other, was going to be the most arduous and perilous of her life.

By the light of an oil lamp, with the tropical deluge drumming overhead, she wrote to her husband: " The whole width of the world has passed under us, except this broad ocean. I shall be glad when we have the hazard of its navigation behind us."

On the morning of 2nd July, 1937, the rain stopped. By 9 a.m. the sky over Lae showed patches of blue. Amelia

and Noonan conferred over breakfast. Away to the east
great, black nimbus clouds still sailed, with the sunlight
crashing between them, but available information on conditions for the area between New Guinea and Howland
indicated a general improvement. They agreed to make a
try. If they ran into heavy cloud before the half-way mark,
they would turn back. Both were anxious to reach home
for the Fourth of July—American Independence Day.

At a few minutes before 10 a.m. Amelia, wearing slacks
and a plaid shirt, took her place at the controls and began
her meticulous cockpit check. Noonan fastened his maps
to the chart table and once more checked his chronometers.
He'd been having a little trouble with the chronometers ;
some sort of radio interference had made it difficult for him
to set them with the absolute precision he would have liked.
If the chronometers were not correct to a fraction of a
second, then the position-fixes he took from the stars would
not be accurate.

All calculations in astro-navigation depend on very
exact timing of each " star-shot " by Greenwich Mean
Time. Normally a very slight chronometer error wouldn't
have been serious, for Noonan didn't rely on star observations. He had three other methods of fixing the plane's
position ; by dead reckoning, by the *Electra's* radio-
direction-finder, and by radio bearings sent out by ships
and shore stations briefed to follow their progress. But this
long hop to Howland, across a featureless waste of ocean
where no aircraft had ever flown and even ships were few,
was going to call for the most careful checking and double-
checking. The target, two-and-a-half thousand miles
distant, was only half-a-mile wide and less than two miles
long, and its highest point was only about fifteen feet
above sea level. The slightest miscalculation, which might

LAST HOP TO HOWLAND

not matter on a routine flight, could bring disaster here.
A deviation of just half a degree over such a long trip
would carry the plane more than ten miles off course, and
if visibility were bad at Howland they might never find
the island.

Noonan meant to use star observations as a convenient
check on the position-fixes he obtained by the other
methods. So he had used the waiting time at Lae to re-
set his chronometers as accurately as possible under the
conditions there, and now he believed them to be trust-
worthy.

Amelia, satisfied with the servicing of the machine, looked
at the windsock and decided to take off towards the sea.
To use every foot of the strip, she manoeuvred *Electra*
close back against the inland boundary of trees, held her
on the brakes and opened the throttles. When the engines
were revving strongly, and the tail was beginning to kick
up, she released the brakes. The plane shot forward in a
breakaway start.

But not until the brink of the precipice was within forty
yards did the heavy-laden *Electra* lift reluctantly, a few
inches at first, wings waggling uncertainly. Then her nose
nudged up a little, she rose evenly, gracefully, out over
the sea. And headed east. Towards the distant storm-
clouds.

George Putnam was waiting in the Coast guard radio
room at Fort Funston, California, not far from Oakland.
He had arranged for all flight information to be forwarded
to him there so that he could follow his wife's progress,
move by move. Just two days ago he'd even managed to
talk with her—over a radio-telephone link with Lae.

This would be the last of these lonely, nerve-gnawing

vigils. Amelia was coming home. She had left Lae, she should be at Howland early next morning, July 3rd. A weather report came in from Howland: "Flying conditions excellent." He drank some coffee, black as anthracite, tried to read a newspaper.

Riding at anchor off Howland was the Coast guard cutter *Itasca*. Her orders were to help guide *Electra* in by radio and to provide local weather information. Her skipper, Commander W. K. Thompson, had been given a copy of the radio schedule worked out weeks before: "Earhart's call letters are KHAQQ. Earhart to broadcast her position on 3,105 kilocycles at every 15 and 45 minutes past the hour. *Itasca* to broadcast weather and homing signal on 3,105 and 7,500 kilocycles on the hour and half-hour." It seemed a straightforward, foolproof arrangement.

But seven hours after *Electra's* departure from Lae the *Itasca*, faithfully following the schedule, had failed to contact her. Darkness closed over the tiny island and Thompson signalled the operators manning a U.S. Navy radio-direction-finder unit on shore: "Have you heard anything from KHAQQ?" Back came the answer: "Negative. . . ."

Shortly after 1 a.m., Howland time, Thompson radioed to the Californian Coast guard: "Have not heard signals from Earhart but see no cause for concern as plane is still 1,000 miles away." Then, right on schedule, he broadcast weather information, by both Morse key and voice: "Howland flying conditions excellent; winds from East, at 8 to 13 knots; sea smoothing, ceiling unlimited."

Not until a little after 2.45 a.m. was Amelia's voice heard, faint and "frying" in static, in the radio room of the *Itasca*. "Encountering headwinds . . . cloudy and overcast . . ."—and then it faded. Thompson immediately ordered transmission of a long series of " A's " by Morse key—a homing signal on which Noonan should be able to take a bearing with his radio-direction-finding device. And then he flashed word to California : " Heard Earhart plane at 0248."

At 3.15, the time scheduled for Amelia's next call, only static—like a million whips cracking—broke the expectant silence of the radio room. At 3.30 a.m. *Itasca* again transmitted her weather report and homing signal and Thompson added this short message: " What is your position ? *Itasca* has heard your phone. Please go ahead on Morse key. Acknowledge this broadcast next schedule."

Amelia came through promptly at 3.45, but she was still on voice transmitter and she did not acknowledge Thompson's message. Her voice was ragged, muffled, frighteningly distant. Only snatches of her sentences could be made out. " *Itasca* from Earhart . . . overcast . . . strong headwinds . . . Will listen in on 3,105 kilocycles at hour and half-hour. . . ." There could no longer be any doubt that she was having serious radio trouble.

Thereafter the carefully detailed radio schedule seemed to be abandoned. Amelia kept breaking through the curtain of static at odd times, faintly and abruptly, with brief, only partly-understood messages. In the cutter's radio room tension mounted ; Thompson and the listening sailors realised that somewhere out in the darkness to the west a great electrical storm was raging, and through it the two flyers were battling for their lives.

Shortly after 6 a.m. the dawn broke clear and still over Howland, and hopes rose. Once *Electra* emerged from the bad weather to the west she should have no trouble spotting the island in such fine visibility—unless, of course, she was badly off course. But at 7.42 the voice which suddenly broke through was decidely strained and anxious: "KHAQQ calling *Itasca*! We must be on you now, but I cannot see you. Gas is running low—we've only about thirty minutes left. I've been unable to reach you by radio. We are flying at 1,000 feet. . . ." Sixteen minutes more, then came a much stronger signal: "KHAQQ calling *Itasca*! We're circling, but still cannot see you! Go ahead on 7,500 either now or on schedule."

Thompson signalled back desperately—confirming her message, then transmitting another series of "A's." And now, for the very first time he got a direct response from her: "Receiving your signals, *Itasca*, but unable to get a definite bearing from them. Please take a bearing on us and answer by voice on 3,105 kilocycles." She began to transmit a long series of "A's" in Morse, but before the *Itasca's* eager radio men could line-up on her and at last determine her approximate position, there came another riot of static and the vital signal was drowned out, lost. . . .

Thompson kept trying, and with his officers made a rapid estimate of the situation in preparation for search and rescue operations. It was clear that despite the foul weather between Lae and here—encountered too late for *Electra* to turn back—Amelia had fought on and accomplished the necessary distance of 2,556 miles in the 18 hours since take-off. But somewhere in that black labyrinth of twisting winds and static-clogged ether, not surprisingly she had gone off course.

The strength of her last signal, and her statement in the one before that she had thirty minutes of fuel left, enabled Thompson to calculate that she must now be within a hundred miles of Howland. If she passed to the south,

Two of the greatest pioneers of aviation.

(*above*) October 1926: Alan Cobham's D.H.50 seaplane lands on the Thames
after his 26,000 mile flight to Australia and back.

(*below*) 1930: Amelia Earhart, who later became the first woman to fly the
Atlantic alone.
(*Photos: Radio Times.*)

(*above*) Sir Charles Kinsford Smith, the Australian air pioneer with Sir Hubert Wilkins, the Australian polar Explorer. (*Australian official photo*).

(*left*) Jean Batten, the famous New Zealand pilot arrives in Auckland in 1934 after flying from Great Britain. (*Photo: N.Z. High Commissioner*).

almost certainly she would spot distinctive Baker Island, about 38 miles distant—and that would put her right. So Thompson went to his chart and marked off a square of sea to the north as the primary search area.

At 8.45 Amelia was heard for the last time: "Earhart to *Itasca*. We are in line of position 157-337, repeat 157-337. Will repeat this message now on 6,210 kilocycles. We are running north and south. . . ." But even as she spoke, and the radio-men once more swung the antennae of their radio-direction-finder, desperately probing the air, reaching for her, the signal faded slowly, receding—so that Thompson knew the *Electra* had overshot Howland, and was speeding away from them now, into the wide, empty ocean. The *Itasca* cast off, steamed northward at full speed. And as she went Thomspon transmitted to America this tragic news: "Earhart unreported 0900 hours . . . believe down."

In the Coast guard Station at Fort Funston, George Putnam read this message, looked up at the silent group of officers and reporters and said quietly: "All right, so they're down. But they can't be far from that cutter, and the sea's calm. The *Electra* will stay afloat indefinitely—the empty gas tanks will give her extra buoyancy. All they have to do is sit tight till they're picked up."

His eyes pleaded with them to agree. The reporters nodded, scuffed their feet, avoided his gaze. An officer said comfortingly: "*Itasca* won't be alone for long. We're sending out a seaplane from Honolulu to join in the search, and the battleship *Colorado*, in Pearl Harbour, has been ordered to raise steam."

Putnam forced himself to relax, sat back in his chair and looked out through the big observation window at the smiling summer sky. This, the last wait, looked like being the longest and toughest of all—but everything would turn out right, Amelia was coming home. . . .

All through that day *Itasca* searched the sea north of Howland, without result. The seaplane from Honolulu didn't show up, and early next morning—July 4th—came the explanation; a freak storm of sleet had started ice forming on her wings, forcing the pilot to turn back. But *Colorado* was on her way, and from the Navy's great base at San Diego the very fast aircraft carrier *Lexington* had started out.

The sea and air search for *Electra* became the biggest rescue operation in the history of aviation. The *Lexington's* force of 76 planes painstakingly covered more than 104,000 square miles of water, and catapult aircraft from *Colorado* made low level surveys of every spur of coral rock which broke the surface in that area of the Pacific. But as the days and nights passed, and not so much as a spar was found, a reluctant world was forced to face the desolate truth—that " A.E.," the great-hearted, quick-smiling girl who for five years had been making flying history, at last had been defeated, and was gone.

How this had happened would never be known for certain, but the evidence clearly indicated that she had placed most of her faith in *Electra's* radio-direction-finding equipment to get her into Howland, and when this failed just after the half-way mark—clogged by electrical interference—Fred Noonan found himself with an almost impossible task. The static also prevented him hearing the ships and shore stations which were supposed to give him bearings. Very probably the dense overcast made it impossible for him to get more than an occasional, fleeting glimpse of the stars, and perhaps his chronometers were not as accurate as he believed.

So, of the four navigational systems on which he had planned the flight, all he had left was his dead reckoning track—a method based on pure deduction, in which the position is calculated from the plane's speed and compass course, the estimated force and direction of the wind, and other factors. And he had nothing against which he could check his findings. Add to this the fact that for hours on end, as he bent over his chart table, *Electra* must have been bucking and slewing through storm-roughened air.

Perhaps they missed the little island by only a few miles. But they were flying east, into the glare of a tropical sun newly risen above the rim of the calm, mirror-like sea. Ironically, had it been cloudy at Howland, they might have had a better chance of spotting their destination—they would not have been dazzled by the fierce sunlight, reflecting upwards from the smooth water and spanking off the metal and perspex of the cockpit into their aching eyes. This is a heart-rending thought; they had battled hundreds of miles through a black night of storms, only to be defeated by a clear morning sky. . . .

Why didn't *Electra* stay afloat long enough for them to take to their rubber dinghy? The most probable answer is that Amelia failed to set her down correctly on the water. Ditching is always a tricky, dangerous procedure, even for the most experienced pilot. It is something that cannot be practised, because it involves the loss of an aircraft. And when you try it with your tanks dry, when your motors are dead, or dying, you get no second chance if you misjudge your approach, because you have no power to pull you out of the stall or see you through a nasty bounce.

Flying-boat pilots, who always land on water, will tell

you they'd rather have it choppy than smooth, because when it is smooth, and the sun is shining brightly, it is sometimes very difficult to judge your exact height above it. When you are looking down at a flat, shining, absolutely featureless surface, there isn't much difference between twenty feet and two feet.

So it seems reasonable to assume that *Electra* hit the water hard, broke up, and sank at once. Especially when we remember how desperately tired Amelia must have been and that the prevailing wind was *from the east*, so that in turning into it to make her emergency landing she would have had that fierce, low sun glaring full in her face. . . .

Not until 10th July—a week after her disappearance—was George Putnam persuaded to give up his vigil at Fort Funston. Haggard, filled with a lacerating sorrow, he had not spoken more than a few sentences in the last 48 hours. Now, as friends escorted him to the car that would take him to an empty home, he paused a moment, looking out towards the Pacific, and said very softly : " If she's really gone, then this is the way she'd have chosen . . . Only, it was to have been her last flight, you see. She said absolutely the last one."

Later he made public a letter which Amelia had left, to be opened only if she failed to return.

" Please know that I am quite aware of the hazards," it said. " I want to do it—because I want to do it. Women must try to do things as men have tried. When they fail, then failure must be but a challenge to others."

CHAPTER EIGHT

ADMIRAL OF THE FORMATION FLEETS

THROUGH THE clear June night there moved, like gentle probing fingers, a tension which seemed to come from the far horizons across the Libyan desert.

Italy had been at war just two weeks. After months of uncertainty, dictator Mussolini had ranted and raved his nation into a grim war-partnership with Adolf Hitler. And now the British air force was reaching out to find the weaknesses of the new foe. Those flying "feelers" had spread from Europe across the North African sands towards the Italian garrison town of Tobruk.

There had been several tentative raids and on this warm June night in 1940, far off to the east the tension had already given way to the persistent drone of heavy-laden aircraft. Surprisingly, the imminence of attack did not over-perturb the small band of inexperienced Italian airmen gathered to defend this remote but vital North African stronghold. With the first warning came whispered news that greatly heartened them ; the Governor of Libya would personally lead his pilots in the defence of Tobruk. And the Governor of Libya was Balbo—Air Marshal Italo Balbo.

Forty-four years old, red-bearded, broad-shouldered and merry of eye and voice, Balbo had been a buccaneering giant in aviation between the world wars. In fact he had become a legend among Italian airmen, and a hero to the ordinary folk. Mussolini, jealous of his popularity and

angered by his fearless opinions, quite recently had contrived to " exile " him to Libya—but his fame lingered on.

Balbo, a small merchant's son, had swaggered down from
Ferrara, in the North of Italy, during the first world war as
a wild, bright-eyed youth—to join the Alpini. He won
two medals for valour, and was marked down as a natural
leader of the new, optimistic movement that soon swept
his country—Fascism. He knew little of politics, but he
knew how to command men, and he was a highly efficient
organiser. He believed sincerely this was the best way to
serve his country.

In 1926 he was made Under-Secretary of State for Air—
and his first decision was to learn to fly himself. To such
an adventurous spirit flying was an obvious outlet. From
the start he proved a natural pilot and an earnest student
of all aviation subjects. Once qualified, he set to work to
build up a new air force. He started out with a few old-
style war planes, many of which had been taken from
Germany as reparations, but soon turned his attention to
new types of aircraft and drew round him a team of young
designers and engineers. With the planes they provided
he launched a series of long-distance mass formation
flights never before attempted.

Seasoned airmen in other lands who heard of his plans
predicted disaster. Formation flying, even with small
units of five or six aircraft, imposed great strain and tension
on the pilots, and made navigation difficult and unreliable.
But Balbo trained and drilled his men so well that he was
able to take neat " boxes " of aircraft for hundreds of miles
over Europe—and perform various aerobatics and manœuvres in most perfect unison. His own daring and
stamina inspired his pilots to tremendous endeavour.

It was a brilliant idea. It brought Italian aircraft on to the world market and publicised the tremendous renaissance of Italy under the vigorous, if undemocratic hands of Mussolini and his lieutenants. To Balbo, the gay blade of those years—as to many others elsewhere in Europe—Fascism stood for progress. Nothing, it seemed, could destroy his simple faith in the future of Italy under Il Duce.

In 1928, Balbo led nine fighters on a non-stop flight from Rome to Hornchurch, in Essex, a distance of 1,000 miles—to show his country's air prowess at the R.A.F display at Hendon. The nine fighters flew in tight, impeccable formations, changing positions in the air as smoothly as well-drilled guardsmen on a barrack square.

Later he piloted one of twelve planes that crossed the Atlantic to South America. His reward for this was a gold medal for valour. Then he led an air tour of no less than sixty-one machines round the Western Mediterranean to the cheers and praise of Arabs and Europeans alike.

But his fame truly blossomed in 1933, when as Minister for Air he flew off as leader of twenty-four new seaplanes to Chicago, and landed on Lake Michigan—on the very threshold of the Century of Progress Exhibition. The crowd that greeted the red-bearded " admiral of the formation fleet " and his pilots was estimated at a quarter of a million !

There was something quite unique and lovable about this simple, handsome, laughing hero of the sky. A frank and open character, he was smilingly accessible to all, whatever their rank ; he made no bones about his love for good living ; and perhaps, above all, his patriotic pride in " the new Italy " made many forget the sinister implications of Mussolini's growing power. Even violent anti-Fascists in America and other lands fell under the spell of Balbo's personal charm, and became his friends. So it was that highly placed statesmen in Great Britain and the United States fêted him on his great 1933 flight.

On his return trip to Italy, Balbo—who, despite his easy-going nature, had an eye to meticulous planning— was forced to re-route by the Azores. He wrote later : " This route never appealed to me as the best. First of all, it presented 625 miles more of ocean to cross, and then the stop at the Azores was hazardous, for it was necessary to land and take-off in a virtually open sea."

He had hung on at Shoal Harbour, in Newfoundland, waiting for a favourable weather forecast which would save him from the Azores. None came. He took off just in time to escape a wide stretch of bad weather which was sweeping up to engulf Newfoundland—if he had waited another few hours he would have been trapped for days. . . .

Half-way across to Santa Maria, great cloud banks loomed up and Balbo had to take evasive action. He led his huge formation up to 12,000 feet. There his pilots were confronted by slashing streaks of lightning. Blinded, they found themselves buffeted about by freak winds in a " no-man's-land " of the heavens.

Balbo kept course as best he could. Then suddenly they were in a comparatively clear sky above Santa Maria. And the new danger—the one they had dreaded during the whole trip—lay below, an awesome sight. The open sea waters where they must land were lashed by storm-winds into white-capped fury. It looked impossible—but they had no option. . . .

Balbo led the " run-in." He drew well ahead of his comrades and, as if to give them a full text-book lesson, went through each action slowly and carefully.

His method—worked out weeks before, in case of just

such an emergency—was to go in across wind, with the nose high and plenty of power, and with precise timing set his machine down in a trough between the racing waves. He judged the touch-down perfectly, brought the plane to a stop, pitching in the turbulence. Then he turned in the cockpit to watch the others come in. The drill now was for his deputy commander, the most experienced pilot, to lead the whole formation down, strung out in wide line-abreast behind him, copying his every move.

Balbo's young co-pilot, sitting beside him, was startled when suddenly his chief pointed to an aircraft at the far end of the big formation, then plunged his head into his hands and groaned : " He's going to crash—I know it ! " The co-pilot stared up in amazement : the plane in question seemed to be making a normal, safe approach along with the rest. Several seconds passed, then the machine abruptly turned on its port side, fell away, ripping its port wing into a heaving roller. It disappeared in a great plume of spray, sinking at once, with its crew.

Balbo raised his eyes, stared at the distant plume of spray, slowly shook his head and groaned softly in anger and grief. The co-pilot studied him for a long moment, then asked softly : " Sir—how did you know . . . ? " The red-bearded face, stained with the trickle of a tear, turned to him.

" The fatal weakness always shows long before danger strikes," he said. Even from that distance he had detected a slight shudder of the wings, realised that the nose was a shade too high and the plane's speed just a little too slow— therefore it must stall. Only a pilot of great talent and sensibility could have recognised these errors so soon, and at such range, in those conditions. This tragic incident —the one fatal crash that marred Balbo's most famous and

successful inter-continental flight—ironically is perhaps
the most impressive example of his fine judgment and
extraordinary ability to anticipate danger.

Back in Italy, Mussolini was waiting with a bear-hug of
congratulations, and more medals. But so hysterical was
the welcome of the vast, frantically cheering crowds in
Rome that day in 1933, that Il Duce's beaming smile soon
wilted—he realised, with a twinge of fear, that this hero
Balbo was probably the only man who could become a
rival for supreme power in the nation. Not that Balbo,
for all his success still essentially a simple man, had any
such ambitions—but the dictator must have known there
were others, members of his cabinet, who might try to use
Balbo's popularity to gain increased power and wealth
for themselves. At any rate, it seems clear that from this
time onwards Mussolini did his best to minimise Balbo's
achievements, at length even to discredit him.

And Balbo to some extent played into the dictator's
hands. As the 'thirties wore on and the German-Italian
partnership became more and more obvious to all, Balbo
made no secret of his detestation of the Hitler regime and
his admiration for the British. Slowly, craftily, Il Duce was
able to undermine his rival's popularity.

With innocent loyalty Balbo went on trying to build
Italy's air force, the Regia Aeronautica, into a major striking
force. At the same time, with cunning purpose, Mussolini
quietly played down the progress made and, with empty
words bolstered the reputation of the Italian fleet. Moreover, he saw to it that funds, new machines and equipment
requested by Balbo were delayed or withheld—thus, for
personal motives, depriving his own people of air security.

When Hitler finally showed his murderous hand in
Europe and began his pressure campaign to bring in

Mussolini as a full partner in his aggression, the Italian Government propagandists were given freedom to attack " the anti-German Balbo."

Just before Italy decided on war, and made her dastardly air assault on crumbling, disorganised France, Balbo's reputation was very much under fire and his standing was so low that he was not consulted in the planning of the raids. But there was little fear of the Allies blaming Balbo for the " stab in the back." Mussolini had already branded him as pro-British—had he not but a month or so previously sent a " good luck " message to Winston Churchill ?

Yet Balbo remained a public hero, especially with his pilots. So Il Duce, fearful of dissension and perhaps revolt in his air force, hung back from arresting him. He took the easy way out ; he sent Balbo to Libya as Governor. The brilliant air leader thus was " promoted to obscurity "— at the hour when he should have been leading his squadrons to battle he was grounded, sent to rot in a backwater.

Without fuss Balbo went, and such was his magnetic personality that within weeks he had built up a loyal band of friends among Arabs and Italian colonists. They already knew of his legendary work for the air force. Now they met the man—laughing, friendly, without a single shadow lingering on his character. And fearless, outspoken still.

So it came as no great surprise in Tobruk when the new Governor left his desk, shut up his residence and once more climbed aboard a fighter plane, to lead his men to defend the desert fortress against the British bombers on that clammy June night.

He flew out expecting to find a large raiding force ; the British, he sensed, had tested the defences enough and now were surely ready to strike. But there was no bomber force. There were two R.A.F. planes which had lost their way, and were only too ready at the first sight of trouble to evade direct battle, especially against the speedy, highly manœuvrable Italian fighters. Balbo chased them off, then turned for home. All right—the attack would come to-morrow, or the day after to-morrow. . . .

At his base he circled low to make his landing, and was preparing for the run-in when suddenly, unaccountably, the Italian anti-aircraft guns opened fire ! The other pilots slewed away. Later they testified that it appeared to them that the ground defences were " concentrating on the leader. . . ."

Balbo dived low, twisted and turned brilliantly to avoid the bursting shells. But they kept coming, clawing for him. Clearing the airfield, to avoid buildings, he had to to climb steeply. A shell exploded close under the belly. The fighter shuddered and suddenly lost height. Balbo fought slack, bucking controls. A second shell cut straight through the plane. The nose dropped, it plunged almost vertically and smote the ground with terrible impact. A pillar of flame and smoke, rising in the still Libyan night, marked the last landing place of Italo Balbo.

Was he shot down by mistake, by over-anxious and inexperienced gun-crews who, because he had returned sooner than expected, mistook him for a British raider ? Or was his end in fact an assassination, planned and ordered by Mussolini ? The truth will never be known for certain, but it is significant that for eighteen months after his death the Italian government made no announcement, much less an explanation—then, out of the blue, came a bald statement that Balbo's death had been " a tragic error."

Balbo's contribution to military aviation is acknowledged by the air forces of many nations. In the difficult business of formation flying, he was an audacious innovator. He was the first air-leader to demonstrate that groups of up to sixty aircraft could " keep station " as precisely over long distances in the air as any battle fleet on the sea ; manœuvre as swiftly as smaller units, and bring tremendously increased fire power to bear on air or ground targets. He introduced many new types of formation, new techniques for changing rapidly from one " shape " to another, for splitting up into smaller groups to attack individual targets, and for reforming quickly and smoothly afterwards. Repeatedly, he proved that these tactics could be carried out in all sorts of weather conditions, short of fog or dense cloud.

Among those who followed his example were operational commanders of the R.A.F.'s Fighter Command. During the Battle of Britain men like Douglas Bader and Robert Stanford Tuck persuaded their superiors to allow several squadrons of Spitfires and Hurricanes to merge and operate as single units. Air Ministry experts feared that such large formations would be " unwieldy," but the experiment proved successful and was generally adopted in the victorious fight against the massed German raiders—who also employed " Balbo tactics."

The Italian airman's skill and personal courage in taking his huge fleets of planes over such great and difficult regions of the world, his readiness in middle age to lead the Tobruk pilots into battle, his flair for showmanship, his personal charm, his fearless criticism of Mussolini, his foresight in training methods and battle tactics, the great respect and affection he inspired in his pilots, the simple, sincere love of his homeland which made him " Italy's super-salesman "—all these qualities make Italo Balbo a giant figure in the history of aviation. A hero who had the misfortune to be " on the wrong side," whose early faith in the new, progressive movement called Fascism brought him in the end disillusionment and exile—perhaps assassination.

His is a strange memorial—fashioned by a nation which fought and defeated his beloved Regia Aeronautica. The Royal Air Force pilots who adopted his methods called the new, large formations " Balbos." And still do, to this day.

CHAPTER NINE

THE TRAIL ENDS AT WALKPI

STAFF SERGEANT Morgan, of the U.S. Army Signal Corps, came into the hut breathing heavily, dragging weary feet. In the eerie, tallow-wick light of the early Arctic day his eyes seemed glazed, his face pale and drawn.

He sat down at his radio key by the window and, very still for a long moment, stared out across the wastes of Northern Alaska, thinking out his message. Then slowly his hand went to the key and he began to transmit.

Sergeant Morgan's call from his lonely post at Point Barrow on that August day in 1935, ran to some thirty words—but in a score of capital cities around the globe it spawned deep, black headlines, and in America it plunged millions into shocked gloom.

" Wiley Post and Will Rogers crashed fifteen miles south of here at five o'clock last night," he reported. " Both killed. Have recovered bodies and placed them in the care of Dr. Griest. Standing by. . . ." This terse, unemotional message confirmed the worst fears of the last twelve hours —that America had lost one of her finest and most flamboyant airmen, and with him his friend and passenger, perhaps the most celebrated humorist and " homely philosopher " of the age.

There was a kind of bitter, ironic pattern to this double tragedy. It was as if fate and the elements had conspired to rob America, at one blow, of her two most far-sighted, active and influential aviation enthusiasts. For though the ex-cowpuncher Rogers had never learned to pilot an aeroplane, he spent most of his enormous income on flying, had covered every main commercial air route in the world and " gone along for the ride " on many important flights with various famous flyers. Next to his friend Post— the one-eyed, part-Red Indian pilot who was the first man to fly solo round the world—he claimed to be " the keenest and busiest aviator on the American continent." Certainly no two men had done more to further the development of United States civil aviation, and to increase public confidence in air travel.

Wiley Post, like his Indian forefathers, loved the open air, and a deep, burning wanderlust would not let him rest. Born at Grand Plains, Texas, in 1900, and raised in Oklahoma, as a youth he had roved from town to town, ranch to ranch, job to job. He farmed, worked as oildriller, lumber-man and cow-hand ; sometimes, while on the move, he washed dishes, or chopped wood, in return for a meal.

To one of the little Western townships where he paused in his wanderings, there came one day an air circus. Wiley and his workmates went along on pay-night to see " the stunters." As he watched the small, brightly-painted biplanes loop and roll and dive in mock dog-fights, dip daringly to pluck handkerchiefs from the grass with spikes fastened to their wing-tips, and finally zoom upside down scant feet over the heads of the crowd, Wiley felt something essential in him stir and grow. He knew now, with a surging certainty, why he'd never been able to stay in one job for more than a few weeks—he hadn't been cut out for

(*above left*) Group Captain A. G. " Sailor " Malan, D.S.O., D.F.C.—South African ace.　(*above right*) Group Captain Douglas " Tinlegs " Bader, C.B.E., D.S.O. and bar, D.F.C. and bar.　(*Photos: Imperial War Museum.*)

(*below*) Supermarine Spitfire Mk. IX. A late version of the world-famous fighter, produced to offset the superiority of the F.W. 190 over the Spitfire V. Powered by a 1,600 h.p. Merlin 61 engine, its top speed was 410 m.p.h.

(*Photo: Vickers-Armstrongs.*)

(*above*) Hawker Tempest V. This fast, heavily armed fighter shot or knocked down 638 V.1. flying bombs. Its 2,420 h.p. Napier Sabre engine gave it a top speed of just under 430 m.p.h.　　　　　*(Photo: Hawker Aircraft.*

(*centre*) Messerschmitt Bf. 109 G.2. Over 33,000 Me. 109s were built between 1939 and 1946, more than any other aircraft in history.　　*(bottom)* Focke Wulf Fw. 190A.4. This formidable German fighter with a 2,100 h.p. BMW radial engine had a top speed of 416 m.p.h.　　*(Photos: Imperial War Museum.*

ordinary work, he was meant to be a flyer! He slipped away from his friends, went in search of the air-circus manager.

" Mister, I'd sure like to join your outfit. I'll do anything to start with. . . ."

" Sorry, son. Got nothing suitable right now."

" I told you, anything'll do. Watchman, grease-monkey, ticket-seller. I'll do a week on trial, if you like."

The manager eyed the lean, straight, strong frame and the young, eager face.

" W-e-ll . . . there just *might* be something, come to think of it. You afraid of heights ? "

" I don't rightly know—I don't think so . . ."

" Ride a horse, don't you ? "

Wiley blinked, gasped, grinned widely.

" All my life, Mister. But I don't see . . ."

" Then you're bound to have a good sense of balance. Let's see your hands, boy." Wiley, in a daze, held out big, calloused palms ; on his wrists and forearms the sinews stood out like bell-cord.

" Hmm—yeah, these ought to give you a strong enough grip. Okay, I'll take a chance on you, son. Start to-morrow. Week's trial, then we'll talk about dough."

And so young Post joined the air circus. Not as a watchman, not as a ticket-seller—but as " the Flying Redskin," a death-defying aerial acrobat who walked the wings of the planes high over the gasping crowds, and made several parachute jumps every day !

It was a sudden startling introduction to flying, but he possessed incredibly strong nerves, and the manager had been right about his natural sense of balance. Once he got his breath back, and gained confidence in his ability to do this strange sort of work, Wiley experienced an exhilaration he'd never known before. To be off the ground, to feel the wind slapping his cheeks and tearing at his clothing, the clamour of the engine beating on his ears—at nights he could not sleep for thinking back over these sensations of the day.

Between performances he hung around the parked aircraft, listening to the pilots and mechanics talking—discussing technicalities in the half-secret language of their rite. Mostly they ignored him, but they let him watch and listen as they worked on the engines and airframes, and once one of the airmen let him sit in the cockpit and explained the controls and instruments to him. Wiley was surprised; he had expected it all to be highly complicated, but in fact it seemed perfectly straightforward, common sense. He felt sure that if only they'd give him the chance, in just an hour or two he'd learn to control this fast, nimble steed as completely as any of the spirited mustangs he'd ridden out on the range. . . .

But they didn't give him the chance. After only three weeks, he was paid off. It was then that he discovered he had been only a temporary substitute for the circus's regular wing-walker, who had fallen ill, and now had recovered.

Back to earth, back to trudging the dusty roads—but more unsettled than ever now, more morose and purposeless. Nothing, nobody here on the ground could hold his interest, every fibre of his being yearned to get into the clear blue air again, to become a qualified pilot—but he did not know where or how to begin. A penniless youngster of Indian blood, without proper education or technical qualifications, a rootless wanderer whose occupation at times might, if he were to be brutally honest, be best described by the word " hobo," or " tramp "—what hope had such a lowly, simple soul of ever being able to afford the hire of an aircraft, the cost of fuelling it, paying an instructor, obtaining a licence and all the many other incidental expenses ? Flying was a costly business, a rich man's sport—he must try to rid himself of this crazy, impossible dream, or he would be miserable all his days.

Wiley Post almost certainly would have stayed on the ground, would never have become a pilot had it not been for an accident in an oilfield, years later. He lost an eye, and was paid £400 in compensation.

Friends advised him to be prudent—to bank the money, or invest it safely. Unemployment was rising in the country, and a man who was disabled, even slightly, might find difficulty in getting work. But Wiley knew exactly what he was going to do—he'd never had so much money in his life, and probably he never would again. This was his only chance. He went out and bought an old, somewhat dowdy Lockheed high-wing monoplane. It was destined to become one of the most famous aeroplanes in history—" Winnie Mae."

In a very few hours Wiley was flying smoothly, safely, nervelessly. But when he applied to the authorities for a pilot's licence, he was refused—on medical grounds. Only after days of pleading did they agree to give him a test. There was no more argument—he quickly proved that his deficiency in sight did not detract from his great, natural flying skill.

In 1930 he won the Chicago-Los Angeles Air Derby in nine hours, nine minutes and four seconds. The following year he teamed up with the experienced Harold Gatty to fly around the world. Wiley put his last pennies into the enterprise—if they could complete the trip in ten days,

they would win £4,000. They made it in the record time of
eight days and sixteen hours—and Post, solvent again and
suddenly an international figure, at last was able to give
up " bread and butter " ground jobs and make flying his
full-time profession.

At once he began planning another round-the-world
flight, this time alone. With scrupulous care, drawing on
the valuable experience of his trip with Gatty, he made
his preparations, fitted new equipment and navigational
aids, tested and practised, amended and modified. By
1933 he was ready.

So well-planned was his flight that everything went
precisely according to schedule—until the 1,800-mile hop
from Moscow to Novosibirsk. Over the Ural foothills
he smacked into blinding fog and thick cloud, a wall of
weather that reached from ground level to well above the
ceiling of his aircraft. And as he started to burrow
through, hoping to find clear skies on the other side of the
range, a pilot's nightmare became reality—several of his
instruments, on which in this situation he was completely
reliant, unaccountably failed.

Buffeted by powerful down-draughts, no longer sure of
his height, speed or heading, unable to see anything beyond
the cloud-muffled canopy, muscles cramped and aching
from days of hard flying and nights with little sleep, Post
fought the bucking controls, tried to maintain height and
course using the few basic instruments which still appeared
to be operating. His strong arms and hands, and his
extraordinary sense of balance, somehow held the plane
on something like an even keel.

But the long, lonely battle seemed to last for hours, and
his strength slowly ebbed. Suddenly the cloud ahead
appeared to grow darker, then a black shape loomed up—

something terrifyingly solid. Wiley hauled on the stick with both hands, kicked on the rudder. The plane rose reluctantly, lurchingly, in a climbing turn, and narrowly grazed the jutting rocks of a hilltop.

Drenched in sweat, nearly exhausted, he realised that his altimeter was out of order—he was much lower than the height it indicated. Fortunately the down-draughts were not so powerful here, and he was able to regain some altitude before resuming course.

On and on through the gloom, with no glimpse of the sun or the earth. His head throbbed, his back and limbs grew stiff and numb. He knew he could not last much longer.

This was the greatest crisis of Post's career. Afterwards he admitted : " I believe if I'd had a parachute, I'd have jumped . . . for it seemed quite impossible to get through." But he did get through—scraping over the shrouded mountain peaks into clearer air, reaching his destination with a few pints of petrol to spare. So fatigued that they had to lift him from the cockpit.

By comparison, the remainder of the trip was easy. He completed his global flight in seven days, eighteen hours and 49½ minutes, breaking the record he had set up with Gatty. Of that, 115 hours and 36½ minutes were actual flying time. His average speed was 127.23 miles an hour.

And he was the first man to have flown round the world alone.

Famous and fêted, he could have rested now ; but the old wanderlust still burned in him, he had to keep on the move. So he went on to many new ventures, including an attempt on the world's altitude record. At Akron in Ohio, the one-eyed " ex-hobo " flew higher than any other human had done, reaching the sub-stratosphere, 7.2 miles up.

Though naturally gifted, Post was no " slap-dash," guessing glory-seeker. He worked hard and long to teach himself technicalities, he sought and respected the opinions of experts and he studied every new idea and development. He always planned and practised meticulously before an important flight, trained diligently as a prize-fighter to get himself in the best possible physical condition. And despite his lack of formal education, in time he became an acknowledged authority on all branches of aviation.

Such then was the man who piloted the plane which crashed near Point Barrow, Alaska, on that day in 1935. His passenger was also from the West, also a national figure—grizzled, sly-grinning Will Rogers, a 56-year-old film actor and " extravagant genius," beloved as a great humorist and as a great human being. There had been a time when Rogers was even considered, quite seriously, as a possible candidate for the Presidency of the United States.

Will had started life as a cowboy, and with his homespun wit had risen to become one of the world's most popular entertainers, earning from radio, films and writing something like £200,000 a year, an enormous income for those days. And a good proportion of that money he spent on flying. In breaks between engagements he would travel by air lines to remote regions, and though he never qualified as a pilot he bought various light machines and hired professionals to fly him between Hollywood, New York and other cities where he was due to appear. Even on short trips he seldom went by train or car—his greatest joy was to get into the air, in any sort of weather, in almost any sort of plane.

Once he was flying to attend an important dinner in Chicago with Henry Ford, the great motor-car magnate, when engine trouble developed and the pilot made a hasty, forced landing in a quiet country area. Rogers broke an arm. They walked to a farmhouse, and a local doctor was called. None too gently, he set the fracture, and Will continued his journey by road.

At the dinner that evening he made one of his most brilliant, wittiest speeches—but never once mentioned his flying mishap. He explained later : " It would have been a reflection on aviation." For when it came to flying, the great humorist was completely earnest ; he believed fervently in the future of air travel, in the potentialities of America's growing aircraft industry, and in the need to build up a strong, modern air force to ensure national security. He was constantly trying to make Americans more airminded—a potent, living advertisement for aviation. And it was natural that this knowledgeable, passionate enthusiast should meet and befriend many of his country's leading airmen, notably " rebel general " Billy Mitchell, and the colourful, energetic Wiley Post.

The cowboy and the redskin had much in common. Both were prairie-bred, of humble origin—and despite success, still essentially simple men. Both had flown twice around the world—Rogers by air line ticket, and by " hitch-hiking " on various military and private aircraft—and they shared a strange, Western wanderlust that in this new, venturesome age found its outlet in the air.

For them the aeroplane had taken the place of the horse, and the world's wide open skies were their range. They had become " partners " long before that summer of 1935, when they set out together to blaze a trail across " the top of the Earth "—a new, northern air route to Russia.

The trip had started in an atmosphere of mystery and conflicting reports which, even now, is difficult to understand. The first the public heard of it was a bald statement from the Soviet Embassy in Washington on 6th July, announcing that permission had been granted for Post and his wife to make a flight across Siberia to Moscow. Newsmen found Post curiously reluctant to supply further details. He confirmed that he had applied to the Kremlin for clearance and airfield facilities " to explore the possibilities of a regular, shorter air route over the Arctic ice," but said his departure date was still uncertain and his general plans for the flight " confidential."

Then, from Hollywood, came the strong and startling rumour that Will Rogers, and not Mrs. Post, would accompany Wiley on the trip. Rogers' studios denied this, and the Posts declined to comment.

On 25th July, while the Posts were preparing to take off for a test flight from a Californian airfield, a chauffeur-driven car swung on to the tarmac. Rogers got out, nonchalantly climbed aboard the plane. His luggage—a magazine, and two packets of chewing gum.

The next day all three were in New Mexico, telling reporters they were " just holiday-making." The newspapermen laughed disbelievingly, settled down to watch and wait; but for over a week nothing happened to confirm their settled conviction that this was some strange, pointless conspiracy—that at the last moment Rogers would take Mrs. Post's place as Wiley's passenger on the trans-polar trip.

Then on 5th August, the reporters were baffled by Rogers' abrupt departure—returning alone to Hollywood. The same day the Posts flew north to Seattle. It seemed as if, after all, the rumour was wrong—that the press had jumped to wild conclusions.

But at midnight Rogers left his Hollywood home by a back door, drove to the airport and, heavily muffled and using the name of Williams, slipped unnoticed aboard a plane for San Francisco. Next day he appeared in Seattle and, in company with Wiley, finally admitted that he, and not Mrs. Post, would be flying to Alaska. But for some reason—still unknown—he refused to say whether he would go on from there to Russia. A few hours later Mrs. Post was with the reporters on the tarmac, waving farewell as the two men took off for the Arctic.

On their arrival at Fairbanks, Alaska, Rogers received a telegraphed message from a New York paper offering him a substantial sum for " the inside story." He wired back a typical, dry-humoured " explanation " about pioneering for gold and exploring the possibilities of a scheme " for growing spinach along the coast of the Bering Sea." Then the two friends took off—and vanished into the icy mists of the North.

Soon the mist became fog, and Post could not find landmarks to fix his position. The temperature dropped dramatically, and the motor began to lose power. Wiley was about to turn back for Fairbanks when, unexpectedly, they broke into a patch of clear air and spotted a tiny Eskimo village. The ground was flat, so Wiley landed, identified the village as Walkpi and found it on his chart.

While Rogers played with the Eskimo children, distributing chewing gum, Post worked on the faulty engine. After an hour he had it running smoothly, but by then the white, Arctic fog was drifting in over Walkpi. Will and

Wiley talked with the weather-wise headman of the village, learned that if the fog closed in completely it was likely to remain unbroken for days, perhaps weeks. They frowned at their chart and at the dazzling white, steadily thickening fog-banks, decided they had no option but to continue— to get off while it was still possible to see a few yards of ground ahead.

A last wave to the villagers, and they roared across the flats. But they had climbed only about fifty feet when the motor seemed to falter. The wings rocked, the nose dipped suddenly. The plane plunged almost vertically, crashed into the shallows of a small lake. And as the Eskimos rushed towards the wreck, petrol, leaking on to the surface of the water, burst into deep, dull roaring flames. So intense was the heat, no one could approach within twenty yards.

A runner was sent to Sergeant Morgan's little post, fifteen miles away. The sergeant commandeered a fast launch, raced down the coast to Walkpi. All that was left of the fuselage was a charred, smoking skeleton. The starboard wing had been torn off, and the engine lay buried deep in a half-frozen hummock of moss.

There were registration numbers on the wing, and he knew there would be markings stamped on the engine. But it wasn't necessary to examine these. Several yards from the wreck a body lay, thrown clear by the impact. A brief glance was enough to identify one of the best-known faces in the world, a face the sergeant had so often seen, sly-grinning under a wide-brimmed hat, and blown up to many times life-size on a cinema screen—Will Rogers.

With the help of the villagers, Morgan carried Rogers' remains to the launch. Then they cut through the blackened, twisted wreckage and recovered the body of Wiley Post. With his sad cargo the sergeant sailed back to Point Barrow, to radio the tragic news to the outside world.

Two wandering Westerners, having ridden hard and risen high, had come together to the end of the trail.

CHAPTER TEN

FIRE CLOUD OVER TURIN

THE THIRTY-SIX Whitleys chosen for the job flew from their bases in Southern England to Cliffield Aerodrome, Guernsey, on the afternoon of 11th June, 1940. They were fully crewed and bombed-up, but their fuel tanks had been filled only to " minimum safety " level.

When the pilots looked down on Cliffield's short runways, they understood why they had been kept light on petrol ; the fewer gallons they carried, the less chance of fire if they crashed on landing. Cliffield had been built before the days of the heavy, multi-engined warplane—it seemed that to get a Whitley in there, you'd need a shoehorn. One or two ran out of runway and bumped to a standstill on the grass beyond, yet they all managed it safely. The crews went off for tea—a special treat of strawberries and cream.

But for the man who was to lead the great " marathon " raid there was no time for eating. Wing Commander W. E. Staton, Commanding Officer of 10 Squadron, Bomber Command, went straight to the Operations room to study intelligence reports and weather maps, plan the attack and prepare detailed briefing for his flyers.

" Big Bill " Staton was a domineering figure, well over six foot tall and thickset as an oak. He was a stern disciplinarian, a superbly aggressive commander ; yet most of the time, with his round face, his glinting eyes and warm Derbyshire voice, he seemed carefree and jovial.

Staton had been flying for almost a quarter of a century. He was 17 years old when he joined the Artists' Rifles in 1916. But his war did not really start until he transferred to the Royal Flying Corps, and was sent to France. By the age of 19 he was an ace, with a score of 28 enemy planes destroyed; in one spell of five days he shot down nine. He was awarded the D.F.C. and bar—and, perhaps more important, he had found his life's work as a flyer.

After World War One he was assigned to a variety of tasks. There were air surveys in the Far East; operations against rebel tribesmen on India's North-West frontier; training pilots back in the United Kingdom, and testing the latest machines and experimental models produced by British designers.

Staton did one other job in those between-the-wars years which earns special note. Of all the planes he flew he loved best of all the old F-boats—wooden-hulled, slow but sturdy flying-boats, like the Supermarine Southampton. It was in one of those planes on an October day in 1927 that Staton, with superb airmanship and courage, rescued a leading aircraftman from another "boat" which had crashed into the sea near Calshot, in Hampshire.

The skippers of the F-boats had to be more than pilots, they had to be expert navigators too. Experience in this type of flying, coupled with his splendid war record and distinguished service on other duties, made Staton one of the most knowledgeable "all-round" pilots in the R.A.F. He was a natural choice for leadership of a heavy bomber squadron at the beginning of World War Two.

How right this choice was is shown in official histories of the war in the air.

The work of the bomber crews had none of the glamour associated with Britain's fighter pilots. Theirs was a highly complicated, physically exhausting, mentally gruelling and extremely dangerous task. Staton summed it up forthrightly as " a binding, dirty job."

Staton's squadron—" Shiny Ten "—was one of the oldest in the service. In 1939 it was generally regarded as the crack unit of Bomber Command. Its bombing error was considerably smaller than that of any rival squadron. So accurate was the navigation that its seasoned crews claimed that, even on the darkest winter night, they could " light up any gate-post in England."

This high standard of efficiency earned " Shiny Ten " prominent representation in the force of thirty-six Whitleys, drawn from several squadrons, which now gathered on Guernsey in preparation for the great " marathon " raid.

And what brought the middle-aged Staton to Guernsey as their commander ? Was his glory not from a war long ago ? The reason was in his log-book—a flight made only ten or eleven weeks before. The Sylt raid. Staton had led the 49 planes on that one. There was heavy flak and they dumped their bombs and cleared out. The job took five hours.

But Staton had not returned with his men. He had taken time to study the lie of the land before dropping his load, and he had a look round afterwards, too, just to make sure that the raid had been successful. He arrived home two hours late. His reward—to be the first World War One flyer to be decorated in World War Two. He got the D.S.O.

Staton was aged 41 at the time, one of the oldest operational pilots in the Service. Three months later he was over Bremen. Dodging searchlights, and even taking time to mislead the heavy enemy defence, his plane wove a mad pattern in the German skies for more than an hour. Then he dived through the flak to 1,000 feet to make sure of blasting an oil depot. Six times his plane was hit and one shell did considerable damage. But Big Bill got home safely.

Such was the man who now, on this June day, was to lead the most difficult and hazardous of air operations ever attempted—a raid which, if even partially successful, would lead eventually to a complete reshaping of the R.A.F.'s bombing policy.

It had all been decided at a few hours' notice. Early that day—11th June—Italy had declared war on France and Britain, and Mussolini had issued a bombastic statement about " tying knots in the British lion's tail." Intelligence had given Whitehall ample warning of the Italian dictator's plans for a " stab in the back," and for several days squadrons of twin-engined Wellington bombers had been standing by on French airfields, ready to take off for targets in Northern Italy.

But this plan for a swift blow at the new enemy was thwarted by the French, who claimed that if the British bombers struck from French bases the Italians were bound to retaliate with raids on French towns and cities. In a wave of panic, hundreds of French civilians swarmed on to the Wellington airfields, formed human barriers across the runways and blocked them with cars, lorries and farm carts. The Wellington commanders signalled the Air Ministry : " Unable to take off."

Prime Minister Churchill had responded with curt orders to Group Captain R. M. Field, commander of the R.A.F. bomber forces in France—at all costs the operation must be carried out. Field contacted top French commanders, including General Waygand, but no amount of argument or pleading could alter the French view that any attack on Italy would result in " terrible retribution against Marseilles, Lyons and Paris." Field realised he could get his Wellingtons into the air only by using force against the French troops and civilians who were blocking his runways. On learning this, Whitehall reluctantly agreed that he must cancel the operation.

So the U.K.-based Whitleys had been called in. Turin was the premier target, Genoa the alternative. The distance there and back was well over 1,400 miles, and they would have to cross the most formidable barrier in Europe—the snow-capped, cloud-wreathed Alps.

For some reason the metereological reports were scanty that day but, by and large, the forecast was favourable. Staton worked out flight plans, then ordered his aircraft—" T-Tommy "—to be serviced and fuelled to capacity. While his crews were having their tea, he taxied out to satisfy himself on one all-important point—that it was possible to get a fully-laden Whitley off that short runway.

He opened up his engines and stood on the brakes until the whole machine quivered and the tail jerked, trying to rise. Then he let her shoot forward, throttles at full power. She staggered into the air with only a few yards of runway to spare.

Staton felt confident all his pilots could make it, provided he briefed them thoroughly on the drill for this sort of take-off. But to brief them, he had to get down again, and landing with full tanks was going to be even tougher!

The crews came out of their messes to watch as the Whitley came in on a long, low approach, dangerously near stalling speed. Dipping a wing occasionally, it levelled out short of the field, a few feet off the grass, and Staton added power. He came in with the nose fairly high, clearing a fence by inches, then throttled back.

For one tense moment the starboard wing went down

But a quick, short burst of power—just the right amount
—brought it up again. Then the wheels kissed the very
edge of the runway in a perfect touch-down. " T-Tommy "
braked to a standstill with at least sixty yards of concrete
ahead. The crews cheered Staton when he arrived at the
briefing. If " Big Bill " could do it with a full load of bombs
and petrol, for them, with empty tanks and racks, it would
be " a piece of cake."

Briefing followed the usual pattern, except for the great
distance involved. The aircraft were to make their way to
the target area independently, but if they struck bad weather
there could be no question of making any large detour, for
they did not carry much of a margin of fuel. Captains
could turn back at their discretion.

Over the Alps they were bound to experience icing. If
airscrews or control surfaces became seriously " crusted "
before they were half-way over the peaks, pilots must return
at once and descend into the warmer air over France.
Finally came details of the principal target—the Fiat Motor
works at Turin, which was turning out aircraft engines and
other war materials for the Fascists.

It was still daylight when they took off. Staton's plane
was the first away. He circled and watched the next three
stagger up from that stubby strip of concrete, then as he
set course for the other side of Europe, he remembered,
" I missed those strawberries ! "

Night wrapped its protective velvet around them as they
crossed the French plains. The weather was fairly clear, and
Staton began a slow climb, planning to cross the Alps at
about 16,000 feet. Then suddenly the controls kicked and
bucked in his hands and he realised anti-aircraft shells were
exploding close by. The French had opened fire, probably
taking them for an Italian intruder.

He opened the throttles and, weaving from side to side, climbed away out of the barrage. A minute or two later, at 12,000 feet, his navigator sighted off to one side Geneva. The neutral city was a warm oasis of lights amid the blacked-out Continent, and provided a perfect "fix." They veered off to avoid passing over Swiss territory.

And then, ahead, a sheer black wall loomed; the Alps were buried beneath a tremendous mass of stormclouds.

They knew that this barrier must stretch unbroken for hundreds of miles. It was no use trying to climb above it for that would consume too much petrol and might take an hour. Besides, very probably the clouds were piled up well above the "ceiling" of the heavy-laden plane. They were left with a choice; either they called off and returned to Cliffield, or they tried to bore their way through, hoping it would be clear on the other side.

Staton had never encouraged fear of bad weather, only a healthy respect for the destructive might of Nature's forces. He believed no conditions existed which could not be turned to advantage, especially in wartime.

Therefore, he drove straight into the blackness. Almost at once the plane was knocked downwards and to one side, and he had to wrestle to keep her more or less on an even keel. The wireless went dead due to the violent electrical disturbances, and fireballs danced eerily all round them.

Several times ice formed, but luckily the Whitley threw it off before it became too thick; every few minutes great slivers of it, thrown inboard off the propellers, smacked against the fuselage with a sound like a musket volley.

Then, with breathtaking suddenness they were pitched out of the boiling blackness into a calm sky; far below, between patches of light cumulus, they saw clearly the soft contours of the Po Valley. A bend in the river provided a " fix," and Staton veered to port for the last lap to Turin, losing height gradually.

The city could be seen plainly from a very long way off. There was no sign of defensive activity. Obviously " T-Tommy " was the first raider to arrive. Over the centre of the city Staton saw a single " bag " of cumulus. He flew straight into it at about 8,000 feet and " hung up " two parachute flares inside. When he emerged and looked back, the cloud was glowing a dark, angry red like some fantastic Chinese lantern. He took the plane down to 4,000 feet.

Soon there came the sinister, winking flashes of A.A. batteries. But no black puffs materialised in the air about them, and they felt no buffeting from bursting shells. The Italians must be incredibly poor marksmen—or perhaps they were shooting at the illuminated cloud !

Ten minutes passed and they could see no other Whitley, no bombs exploding. There was no mistaking the Fiat Works and Staton nosed down to 1,000 feet, starting his run at the target. His bombs—2,500 pounds of high explosive and several bundles of incendiaries—overshot the main building and smashed a long, low structure just beyond. Immediately widespread fires flared up. The flames were an unusual colour, light greenish-blue. Staton's guess—later confirmed by Intelligence—was that he had hit the acid tanks.

As they circled, another part of the factory erupted in bright orange flames. A second Whitley had arrived. Staton waited over the city, on the lookout for fighters, and saw four more bomb-loads hit the works, making a tattered cloak of the Italian night. Then he climbed slowly, in readiness for the return over the Alps.

The trip back was another bruising battle. This time the ice formed faster and thicker, and the plane flopped down on to the cushion of still, warmer air over France just in time. As the last ice melted and broke away, the Whitley —rid of her bomb-load and much of her fuel—grew wonderfully buoyant. Smoothly and swiftly she flew the rest of the night away. They reached their home base, Cliffield, in broad daylight and clear summer weather.

Within the next few minutes they were able to make a preliminary assessment of the results. No aircraft had been lost, but of the thirty-six Whitleys which had set out, only thirteen had got through beyond the Alps. The others had been forced to turn back by very severe icing and the electrical disturbances.

Yet the savage weather had, in Staton's own phrase, been " turned to advantage." The Italians had been confident that no bombers could penetrate the thundery bastion on their northern frontier, so their fighter squadrons had been caught unprepared. Not one Whitley had so much as glimpsed an enemy aircraft over Turin or Genoa—the secondary target, which had been attacked by the last two or three raiders.

The average time in the air for the thirteen planes which had completed the mission was approximately nine hours. Well over 30,000 pounds of bombs had been dumped on the targets.

But the most important result of that long night's work was not immediately evident to the weary crews. Only a handful of experts at the Air Ministry, and the War Cabinet, realised that their determination, their skill in navigation and aircraft handling amid dreadful conditions, had opened the way for a bold campagin of long-range bombing which, in the months ahead, would weaken the Axis morally and materially.

After " de-briefing " on that morning after the first

" marathon," Big Bill was preoccupied with less exalted thoughts. He strode into the mess and told a steward : " I need a big breakfast—I missed my tea yesterday ! " The steward grinned—and so did Staton—as a large helping of strawberries and cream was laid on the table.

And later ? Staton fought in the Far East, and in 1943 was captured by the Japanese. But in 1945 he came home, and in 1949, at the age of fifty, he went to a training command as an Air Vice-Marshal. On his chest he wore the high tokens of bravery ; the ribbons of the C.B.E., D.S.O. and bar, M.C., D.F.C. and bar.

CHAPTER ELEVEN

ONE SEPTEMBER DAY

THE ENEMY bombers approached London from the South-East, flying at about 22,000 feet. As the wailing of the sirens rose to mingle with the malicious drone of the raiders' engines, people looked up and saw ugly clouds of aircraft besmirching the immaculate September sky.

The attack was one of the strongest yet mounted by the Luftwaffe in daylight. It seemed that the enemy had put every bomber they possessed into the air, intending that this day—September 15th, 1940—should give Germany undisputed mastery of the skies.

As usual, to hold the whole force close together, the slowest aircraft had been put in the lead—a bunch of about fifty Heinkel 111's. Behind and a little to the side of these, followed large formations of Dornier 215's. Finally, throttled back to a little above stalling speed in order to keep station, came a solid phalanx of about forty fast and formidably-gunned Junkers 88's.

Between 5,000 and 8,000 feet above the bombers, the escorting fighters fussed—a squadron of Me. 110's and another of Me. 109's. In all there were probably about 200 " bandits " heading for the densely-populated centre of London.

It was a hot, windless day. For weeks on end the weather had been perfect, the kind of old-fashioned English summer people had dreamed about before the war, but hardly ever seen. Now, just when rainclouds or gales would have provided respite for the island's severely outnumbered defenders, day after day Britain awakened to bright sunshine.

The raiders' plan was to drop their bombs all together in a comparatively small area, thus blowing a hole in the hub of the city. They reached the southern outskirts unchallenged and turned for the run on to their target. It seemed now that nothing could stop them.

But far below, the sun glinted on metal. Up out of the indigo haze that lay over the sprawling metropolis climbed a wing of R.A.F. fighters—two squadrons of Spitfires, one of Hurricanes. Thirty-six young men rising into the vast blue battleground to face the Nazi armada.

Stencilled on the fuselage of the leading machine of this all too small force—a Hurricane—were fourteen swastikas : curt epitaphs for German aircraft destroyed by its pilot, the leader of the wing, Squadron Leader Roland " Bob " Stanford Tuck.

At this period of the Battle of Britain the Air Ministry's policy opposed the building of " ace " reputations. The emphasis was on teamwork. Perhaps one of the reasons was that people are inclined to credit an " ace " or hero with god-like luck ; he becomes a mascot of success, and like an ancient god must never die if his worshippers are to be saved from despair.

Only three months before that September day there had been another god-like hero of the air, J. E. " Cobber " Kain, a lean, laughing six-footer from New Zealand. The R.A.F.'s first ace of World War Two, his exploits fired the imagination of the whole western world. No wonder ; once, supported by only one other aircraft, he had attacked seven enemy bombers—and chased them back to Germany.

For that he was awarded the D.F.C. Then there was the time he destroyed two Messerschmitts and was himself shot down. Wounded, and with his plane in flames, he baled out only half-a-mile from the German lines, but got back to his squadron, where the doctors found twenty shrapnel wounds in his leg.

God-like luck it seemed.

In March, 1940, Kain was to return to England for special duties, and to marry a beautiful English actress. He looked round his fellow-officers on the edge of the runway at Blois airfield.

"One more beat-up, lads," he called cheerfully, climbed into his Hurricane and was off—on a wild display of aerobatics, flashing across the airfield mere inches off the grass, the fighter rolling and twisting like a demented fish.

Minutes later the cheers and laughter died on the lips of his watching colleagues. Kain could not get out of a low roll. The plane's wing touched the ground. A rending, splintering crash. Kain—the symbol, the god-like indestructable—lay smashed and lifeless in the midst of the mess.

So after that, no more immortal symbols—the emphasis was on teamwork. But it proved impossible to keep secret the spectacular personal gallantry and outstanding skill of other pilots, men like Douglas Bader, the South African "Sailor" Malan, and Bob Stanford Tuck.

At twenty-four, Tuck was a veteran, a "grey-beard" mentor and father-confessor to the fledgling pilots of nineteen and twenty. He was also, despite official censorship, a national legend. It wasn't that he sought publicity in any way—it just seemed that every time he got off the ground he made the kind of news that pumped fresh confidence into his countrymen, and that newspaper correspondents would break rules to print.

Tuck had joined the R.A.F. in 1935 after a brief spell in the Merchant Navy. Long before the outbreak of war, he was one of the first service pilots to fly the Spitfire. The sensational new monoplane, with its eight machine-guns, its incredible manœuvrability, high ceiling, and tremendous speed, fired the exuberant Tuck with a host of ideas for revising air tactics. Nobody listened to him at the time, but later his schemes were to bring immense profits.

He first saw action in May, 1940, over Dunkerque, as a Flight-Commander with a new Spitfire squadron. His comrades heard him whooping with glee over the radio as he led his section into the middle of a large formation of Me. 109's. The squadron destroyed eleven for the loss of one Spitfire which crash-landed on the beach. Tuck was credited with one " kill." That same afternoon, while on a second patrol over the same area, he shot down two Me. 110's. He followed up that " bag " of three for the first day's combat with a couple of Dornier 17's the next day, and another of the same type on the third morning. Six in three days. " This is the most fascinating occupation in the world," he wrote in a letter to his parents at Walton-on-Thames, Surrey.

A fraction over six feet tall, whip-thin, whip-strong, dark and lithe and elegant as a matador, Tuck seemed to embody all those elusive, incongruous qualities which make a great fighter pilot. He had tremendous energy, he was an excellent marksman and a gay and popular character in the mess. In the air, even in the midst of combat, he was always astonishingly calm and workmanlike ; in a job where the blood was apt to boil, and hatred could blur the vision, he remained a fastidious, methodical, ice-brained crafts-man.

Here then was the man who led the thirty-six fighters up to the defence of London that September afternoon. This time he flew a Hurricane, for a few days before he had taken over leadership of a new squadron, 265. His pilots had flown three previous patrols that day, without incident. For many weeks they had been averaging about four-and-a-half hours' sleep a night, and snatching their meals out of " hot-boxes " brought to them at the flight dispersal huts. They were youngsters with haggard faces and wary eyes.

Now, on the fourth " outing " of the day, everything was against them. There was no time to gain altitude or get the sun behind them. If they were to break up the enemy formation before it reached its target, then they must attack from beneath. This meant there could be no surprise, that the German fighters would have the advantages of height and, because they could dive to the attack, higher speed. Tuck ordered the wing to join up in a loose formation—a method of attack he had himself introduced, because he believed tight, "copybook " formations forced the pilots to concentrate too much on watching their comrades' wing-tips instead of looking out for the enemy.

After months of argument Tuck, and a number of other experienced leaders, had managed to get the idea accepted that fighters should operate not in squadrons (units of as few as twelve machines) but in wings (three, sometimes four squadrons flying as a single, fairly widely-deployed pack). Once in combat the fighters operated in pairs, one attacking, the other covering his tail. So far as possible they maintained some sort of general formation so that they could re-group quickly at an order from the wing leader. (These tactics had been introduced before the war by the great Italian airman Italo Balbo—and Tuck, an avid student of every development in aviation, had devoured all available reading matter on Balbo's theories and work.)

But this time matters did not work out that way. The planes which had been the last to take-off could not catch up with the leading section, and the formation was dangerously stretched out. Yet Tuck and the other leading machines dared not throttle back to wait for the laggards : if they were to catch the raiders while they were still over the southern fringe of London, they must use everything in their engines, climbing on at full power. . . .

Thus, when the leaders came up under the bombers and Tuck called his pilots into line-abreast, only about seven machines were able to draw level with him for the all-important opening burst. The German fighters, of course, had seen them coming all the way. The 109's peeled off and came screaming down through the closely packed formation of Ju.88's, which were still well out of range of the British fighters.

Tuck kept on, ignoring the plummeting fighters, and got a Junkers lined up in his sights. As the bomber's silhouette grew steadily larger on the ringed glass, a 109 came hurtling down on him, wicked little flames flickering along its wings as it sent a stream of fire close over his canopy. Now he couldn't ignore the danger. He was forced to slam the stick over and break off his attack.

He made a steep turn, climbing away, with his Number Two, Sergeant Ronnie Jarvis, following close behind. All at once and straight ahead he saw the Me. 110's making a slow, wide turn, to face the other British fighters which were now drawing near the tail end of the bomber stream.

He picked one out, closed swiftly and pressed the firing button. The enemy machine shuddered, fell lazily out of position and burst into flames. The rest of the formation began to disintegrate. Tuck swung round after a He.111 which had suddenly turned and was fleeing for home. But down on him, almost vertically and very fast, came a Me 109. Its fire went wide, and it plunged past him before he could reply. But he knew there would be another following—the enemy, like the British, operated in pairs.

Tuck craned his neck and, sure enough, spotted the Number Two following its leader down. But this second Messerschmitt pilot either lost his nerve or became confused, for suddenly he pulled out of his dive and turned in front of the Hurricane, flying into the centre of Tuck's sights as obligingly as a homing pigeon to its loft.

A long burst. The machine rolled on its back and went down. Tuck turned in search of more prey, but the battle was over. The fleeing Germans were jettisoning their bombs at random. Most of them would explode harmlessly in open country. The tiny British force, by sheer resolution and accurate shooting, had turned back an armada.

Back at base Intelligence credited Tuck's squadron with the destruction of five enemy planes, and the ground crew stencilled two more swastikas on their leader's aircraft—bringing his official total at that time up to 16.

The events of that September afternoon serve to illustrate how Tuck's methods during the Battle of Britain, his example, and his cool, almost casual personality contributed to the eventual triumph of " The Few."

Tuck survived. By the end of 1941, when the Battle of Britain was won and Fighter Command was able to go over to the offensive, he was a Wing Commander holding the D.S.O., the D.F.C. and two bars, and officially credited with twenty-nine " kills."

The next year, in January, Tuck was out on a low level offensive patrol over France when a German shell blew most of the engine out of his Spitfire. He spotted a long, flat field on the outskirts of Boulogne and went in to make a crash-landing. Not until he was flattening out, four or five feet off the grass, did he realise that there were guns all round the field. At the far end, straight ahead of him, he could see four 20mm. pieces mounted on the back of a huge lorry. He was landing smack in the middle of the enemy A.A. battery which had shot him down . . . !

The crew of the multiple 20mm. had depressed the sights, and they opened fire on the crippled fighter, now only a few hundred yards away. Nobody shot at Tuck and got away with it. Not even when his plane was dying, and he was only a few inches off the ground. He shoved the nose forward, pressed the firing button—and blew the gun-crew off their lorry.

The Spitfire, slowed by the recoil of its guns, thumped down heavily on the field and Tuck was knocked out for a few seconds. When he came to Germans were running towards him from all directions. Rough hands seized him, twisting his arms, and propelled him across the field to the wreckage of the gun lorry.

He looked down, saw the mangled bodies of the gunners he had killed with his last burst, and waited for retribution. He was quite sure they meant to string him up from the nearest tree. But to his amazement, suddenly his captors were laughing, pointing at the back of the shattered lorry. Tuck saw now that by an astounding fluke one of his cannon shells had gone right up the barrel of a gun, splitting it open, like a half-peeled banana. Such marksmanship evidently appealed to the Teutonic mind. A gunner clapped his back: " Goot shot, Englander! " Again, it seemed, his marksmanship had saved his life.

Tuck later escaped from a German prison camp into Russia, and turned up in Italy in the spring of 1945. To-day he has his home in Kent. Under the very skies where so many of his hardest battles were fought, he lives quietly, a successful mushroom farmer.

CHAPTER TWELVE

DUEL IN THE MIDNIGHT SUN

THEY WERE flying over dreary wastes of ocean far inside the Arctic circle when a faint elongated blob materialised on the radar screen. According to the Intelligence reports no Allied vessels were anywhere near this area. The " blip " was so large that they thought it must be a destroyer.

Cruickshank said crisply : " Stand by," eased back his throttles and put the nose down. The wide-winged Catalina flying-boat—" Y-Yorker "—went into a shallow, graceful dive, cutting through occasional banks and streamers of clean, white sea fog.

The gunners peered out over their sights, straining their eyes in the dim, tallow-wick light of the Arctic's " perpetual dusk," tentatively swinging and depressing their guns while the navigator-bomb-aimer, Flying Officer J. C. Dickson, called out the decreasing range.

At about 800 feet they emerged from a fog-bank and saw their quarry slightly to starboard about half-a-mile ahead. It wasn't a destroyer. Cruickshank's precise Scots voice came clearly over the inter-comm :

" U-boat ! Right, lads, we're going in. . . ."

It was one of the latest types of enemy submarines, about five times the tonnage of the standard U-boats. The conning tower bristled with heavy machine-guns, and 37mm.

and 20mm. anti-aircraft cannon were mounted on the deck fore and aft.

There had been a time, earlier in the war, when a German submarine automatically crash-dived on sighting an Allied aircraft. But now—in July 1944—most U-boats remained on the surface and fought it out, often with considerable effect. This large, well-armed vessel was a truly formidable enemy and Cruickshank knew he must try to make good use of the element of surprise to get in the first blow.

The Catalina banked steeply to starboard, straightened out and dived on her target. Dickson called : " Good luck, Skipper ! " in the cheerful, almost gleeful, tone that so typified his personality, then hurried forward from his navigation table to take charge of the apparatus which aimed and released the depth charges.

Up in the nose of the plane Flight Sergeant Harbison, the engineer/air-gunner, lined up his sights. It would be his task to try to mow down the Germans as they scrambled to their guns, thus smothering the anti-aircraft fire.

Flight Sergeant John Appleton, the wireless operator/ air gunner, and Sergeant S. I. Fidler—making his first trip in a Catalina—manned the waist, or " galley " guns. They stood amidships, with the big " blister " canopies wide open and the icy wind tearing at their clothing, ready to spray the U-boat's deck as they passed overhead. In a matter of seconds the crew of " Y-Yorker," literally a flying warship, were poised at battle stations.

Their bodies were tense and their lungs heaved jerkily, but this was due more to eagerness and excitement than to fear. For this moment they had waited many months— monotonous months of long, exhausting, utterly uneventful patrols.

The air-sea war that Coastal Command had to fight was always exacting, seldom spectacular. The work was entirely unrelated to the screaming turmoil of fighter sweeps over France, or the fiery fury of bombing raids on Germany. Theirs was a world apart from the rest of the Royal Air Force; in fact, since 1941, Coastal Command had operated directly under control of the Admiralty. There could be no Allied victory unless the convoys got through to British ports. Coastal Command was there to help them to get through.

Now, in the last hours of 17th July, 1944, Catalina " Y-Yorker " of 210 Squadron seized a hard-earned opportunity and, by the light of the " midnight sun," dived to the kill. From here on much depended on the skill, courage and coolness of the skipper.

Flying Officer—later Flight Lieutenant—John Alexander Cruickshank was a tall, long-jawed and somewhat morose Scot of twenty-four. Before the war he had worked in a bank in his home town, Edinburgh. " Jock " Cruickshank had never been an outstanding officer. Throughout his training—under the jurisdiction of the United States Navy at the air " university " of Pensacola, Florida, where he first flew Catalinas—his instructors had used words like " average," " reliable," " conscientious " in their progress reports. He was, by his own admission, " a plodding Scot —and a bit of a dour one at times."

But the crews who flew with him on operations—at first from Gibraltar, then later with 210 Squadron from Sullom Voe, in the Shetland Islands—soon discovered that this quiet young man with the neat black moustache was a considerate, thorough and highly efficient captain. It was strange that Cruickshank, who preferred the solitude of his quarters to the boisterous atmosphere of the mess, should choose as his closest friend the effervescent, widely popular navigator, "Dicky" Dickson.

"Y-Yorker" levelled out about 100 feet above the water and Harbison opened fire from the nose. But the Germans must have heard the plane's engines some time before; already they were manning their deck guns, and now they filled the air round the "Cat" with bullets and shells. The advantage of surprise was lost.

In the best "copybook" style, Cruickshank continued his run-in—that most perilous of manœuvres, when the reflexes kick and the instinct clamours for evasive action; when, against all human nature, the attacking pilot must fight to keep his aircraft straight and steady, though the sky ahead and all around him is erupting death, and exploding shells set the controls bucking crazily in his hands.

The American-built Catalina was an invaluable aircraft in many respects. With her exceptional endurance in the air—well over sixteen hours—she was ideal for long-range patrol work. But her top speed in straight and level flight was only ninety knots (just over 100 m.p.h.) which, combined with her huge wing-span, made her a very good target for hostile gunners, especially when making a low level attack.

Grimly, dourly, Cruickshank held "Y-Yorker" on her course of destruction. And as he bore down on the U-boat, the Germans' fire seemed to become much less accurate. Agonising seconds dragged by while Cruickshank flew on relentlessly; it is a remarkable fact that up until the instant that the "Cat" sedately passed over the U-boat they seemed to have completely escaped the slightest damage.

Dickson, crouching over his aiming gear close behind the first and second pilots, yelled in dismay. He had pressed the release button, but nothing had happened! The release mechanism was jammed—their depth charges had " hung up ! "

It was then that they began to suffer. A stream of machine-gun bullets ripped into the tail unit and after-hull, and jagged hunks of shrapnel smashed through the port side of the fuselage. " Y-Yorker " yawed and staggered sickeningly as she turned steeply to climb away, her wing-tip only a few feet above the waves.

From the waist position Appleton and Fidler blazed away—first downwards, then directly backwards. But the skipper's evasive action threw them off the target after only a few seconds.

" Check the gear," Cruickshank ordered. " We'll have another go at her ! "

From the start of the second run-in the Germans, filled with new confidence, kept up a fast and well-directed fire. As the " Cat " dived Dickson reported he could find no fault in the release gear—they could only hope it would work next time. . . .

" Right," said Cruickshank. " Make sure nothing's burning. Anybody wounded? What about the guns? " All this methodical " pilot's handbook " talk while they continued to fly in through the full blast of the enemy barrage ! In quick succession the answers came over the inter-comm. Nobody was hurt, there was no fire and all the gunners had reloaded.

But half-way through the second run-in a stream of shells smashed through the aircraft, and directly after this a shell came in through the bottom and exploded. Dickson was blown backwards into the waist. He lay limp and twisted among the empty cartridge cases at the gunners' feet.

Fidler stooped to tend him. At that instant there came a thunderous roar and a section of the after-hull burst into flames. In a few moments the whole inside of the plane was filled with smoke and acrid fumes.

Up front, Harbison screamed with pain as slivers of shrapnel pierced his legs, and the second pilot, Jack Garnett, was thrown clean out of his seat when the windscreen in front of him disintegrated. An icy wind howled through, clearing the smoke, but fanning the flames.

Johnnie Appleton was lurching about, dazed, trying to pick pieces of shrapnel out of his right hand. He had to give up, because blood, streaming from another wound in his head, ran into his eyes.

All this time the skipper somehow kept the ship heading straight for the U-boat. Except when shells struck the aircraft, so that she jarred like a car hitting deep ruts, he held her wonderfully steady.

With about a hundred yards to go he glanced round and realised there was nobody to release the depth charges. But Garnett, bleeding in several places, had clambered back into the second pilot's seat. Grasping the situation, Garnett took over the controls and held the aircraft on course while his captain leaned back and—just in time— pressed the release button.

There was no chance to aim properly, but Cruickshank's judgment was true and this time the release gear worked perfectly. The wounded Harbison, lying prone in the nose gun-compartment, forgot his pain as he watched the depth charges go forward and downward, tumbling awkwardly as dustbins, and enter the water close by the U-boat.

The instant before the vessel passed out of sight beneath the plane he saw the surface of the sea quiver and thick, white columns begin to rise. Finally, the sub's steel deck buckled, cracked open; there was a searing flash of red flame and a violent explosion inside—probably the torpedoes detonating!

There could be no doubt that the U-boat was destroyed, and that all her crew had perished in the fiery blast. But the victors of the air-sea duel were in a desperate condition.

Appleton, having staunched the flow of blood from his head wounds, took a fire extinguisher and, aided by Fidler, managed to put out the flames aft. In the cockpit Garnett suddenly noticed that Cruickshank's face was leprous white, and a corner of his lip was trapped between clenched teeth.

" You all right, Skipper ? " Garnett asked. There was no answer. Garnett went aft and said to Appleton : " I think the Skipper's been hit."

Appleton told him Dickson was dead, killed instantly by a shell which must have exploded only inches from him. They found the first aid kit and went forward.

Garnett took over the controls and Cruickshank indicated to Appleton a jagged tear in his trouser leg. The Flight Sergeant started to cut away the material, but suddenly the Skipper fainted and slumped forward.

With Fidler's help Appleton got Cruickshank back on to the 'midships bunk—the only one that had not been destroyed by fire. They discovered dozens of deep leg wounds, realised that he must have lost a dangerous amount of blood. Obviously he had been wounded early in the second run-in, but had made no mention of it.

After dressing the leg wounds Appleton noticed dark patches on the front of Cruickshank's shirt. He cut away the material and discovered that the skipper's chest was covered with deep gashes; in at least two places it was clear that shrapnel had pierced the lungs.

And then the Skipper opened his eyes. " What about Dickson ? " he asked. Appleton shook his head sadly, and prepared to administer morphia, but Cruickshank stopped him. " I want to stay awake, Johnnie, in case there's more trouble."

With Garnett at the controls and Fidler navigating they started on the five-and-a-half hour flight back to base—600 miles away. " Y-Yorker " was shuddering and wallowing, threatening to founder under them. The comparatively less experienced second pilot did his best to nurse her along, but soon he began to lose height.

After an hour or so Cruickshank heaved himself up and swung his bandaged legs over the side of the bunk. He wanted to go forward and help Garnett. Only with great difficulty did Appleton persuade him to stay where he was.

Cruickshank lay down again, and now the palsy of shock seized him. The violent trembling stretched and twisted his wounds and he felt himself swallowed in a red fog of pain. Beating pain, crawling pain, pain that consumed like fire. Yet he fought to remain conscious, and again refused morphia.

To lighten the aircraft they jettisoned some of the non-essential gear, and after that Garnett, though sick and dazed from his own wounds, managed to maintain height.

As they flew south-east towards the Shetlands the sky darkened to the colour of fractured iron. They were leaving the area of " perpetual dusk," crossing the Arctic Circle, and it was still black, inhospitable night on the other side.

When the last light faded Appleton came up beside Garnett. The second pilot glanced back at the big holes in the bottom of the hull which they had tried to plug. "It's not going to work, Johnnie," he said. "As soon as we land the water will start coming in fast. We'll have to run her up on to the beach or we'll sink in just about two minutes."

It wanted a little over an hour till dawn when at last the battered plane reached Sullom Voe. Somehow Cruickshank sensed they were over base. He had stopped trembling now, but he was so weak from loss of blood he could not talk above a whisper.

"I'm still giving orders," he croaked. "Help me up to my seat." He knew Garnett had made very few night landings in a Catalina, and this wreck would be difficult to set down even in broad daylight. Fidler and Appleton had to carry him forward.

"Ditch the guns," he said. "And everything else that's movable."

Appleton and Fidler opened a " blister " and tossed out into the inky blackness the machine-guns, ammo and all the detachable equipment that remained. The Skipper caught a glimpse of white-capped waves far below. The water was choppy. He ordered Garnett to circle base; they would wait until it was light before tackling the last obstacle which lay between them and safety.

When it was sufficiently light to see the narrow stretch of water which was their runway, Cruickshank stretched out his hands and took the controls. "We'll do this together, Jack," he told Garnett. "But if I pass out, it'll be up to you."

The crippled " Cat " was liable to stall easily, so they made their approach at a higher speed than usual. They levelled out a few feet above the water and flew on, wings rocking a little, until they were nearly opposite the shore station. Then, bracing themselves, they eased back the throttles and let her settle.

The instant the keel hissed on the water they added power again to hold her before she could settle too deeply. Like a speedboat she sped across the dawn-lit bay in a cloud of spray half-sailing, half-flying. By revving up one engine and throttling back a little on the other they managed to turn her in towards the beach.

Water boiled in at half a dozen places, and soon it was swirling round their ankles. She began to slow, settle deeper. Rescue launches started out from the shore to meet them, sure that they would sink before reaching the beach.

"Full throttle!" Cruickshank ordered.

The two big, sturdy Pratt and Whitney engines strained to full, roaring power, and the spray whipped up by the propellers came through the broken windscreen, stinging their faces, blinding them, making them splutter and gasp for air.

They could feel now that the nose wanted to go down. That would be the finish. Garnett locked his arms round the wheel yoke and pulled backwards with all the strength he had left.

"Y-Yorker," pitching increasingly and filling rapidly, clawed her way across that stretch of rough sea. On the last 100 yards only her screaming propellers kept her afloat, though they were taking as much water as air. She floundered on to the beach with seconds to spare.

The squadron medical officer gave Cruickshank a blood transfusion as he lay on a stretcher on the slipway. This time he accepted morphia and sank into blissful unconsciousness.

At hospital they found he had no fewer than seventy-two wounds. But after weeks of operations he recovered to go to Holyrood Palace, in his native Edinburgh, and receive from King George VI the nation's highest award for gallantry, the Victoria Cross. At the same investiture Flight Sergeant Garnett received the Distinguished Flying Medal for his part.

After the war, unable to shake off " notoriety," Cruickshank left for Rangoon, to work in a bank there. He has always insisted that he did no more than his duty, and that wider recognition should have been given to the members of his crew—in particular to the skill and gallantry of his navigator and great friend, Flying Officer Dickson, the man who guided them accurately through the fog-banks to their quarry.

Whatever this quiet, modest man has said, his own conduct was outstandingly heroic, a glorious example to his colleagues. Captains of Coastal Command like John Cruickshank, in partnership with the Royal Navy, slowly wore down the enemy and in the end denied him the element in which Britain had ruled supreme throughout five centuries.

CHAPTER THIRTEEN

HEAD IN THE CLOUDS

SHORTLY BEFORE four p.m. Cunningham climbed into his Beaufighter with his radar-navigator, Rawnsley. It was perhaps one of the worst days ever to mock the avouched merriness of May in England; matted black clouds came lumbering down from the nearby hills and Middle Wallop was blurred by sheeting rain.

John Cunningham's weather, this. Most R.A.F. fighter pilots revelled in clear skies and strong sunlight, but the short, blond, baby-faced Cunningham was a lurker in the shadows, greedy for gloom—a superbly efficient killer in the innermost caverns of the clouds and the darkest recesses of the night. Britain's number one night-fighter ace, in fact.

Many tall stories were told about him. For instance, newspapers reported that he ate pounds of carrots, and stayed in his room between dawn and sunset with the blinds drawn, in order to sharpen his vision. And it was said that as visibility faded his blue eyes began to shine and acquired a greenish hue—" Cat's Eyes Cunningham," they called him, " the man who hates the sunlight."

Exaggeration, propaganda. But it was indisputably true that at 25, at the peak of his strange yet brilliant career, this destroyer of the darkness could rise into the foulest sky, stalk a fast and wary prey and get into position to make his kill without once lifting his gaze from the instrument panel—guided only by Ground Control's radioed messages,

Rawnsley's murmured headings and the faint, pulsating "blip" of his radar screen. In addition to swiftness of reflex, sureness of marksmanship, high courage and all the other usual qualities of a great fighter pilot, Cunningham possessed a quick, logical, scientist's brain. And always he was relaxed, cool, imperturbable.

His eyes certainly seemed to be shining now, as he strapped himself into his seat and peered out through the streaming windscreen. The clouds were thickening, the light was fading, definitely fading. Somewhere up there, tunnelling through the murk, the crack Luftwaffe unit K.Gr 100 was making its first "blind" bombing run on Britain. According to the Intelligence warning the Germans were equipped with a new radio aid for flying in cloud—though just what this was, and how it worked, nobody on this side of the Channel knew. But surprises were expected, so Cunningham—with his very special talent and experience—was going up ahead of the other defenders to "investigate."

Carefully he checked his treasure-trove of instruments, took off, rose swiftly. Within seconds the Beaufighter was swallowed up in the vast, sodden gloom.

Inside their little perspex capsule, burrowing through the soupy strato-cumulus, Cunningham and Rawnsley flew and navigated entirely by their instruments and the directions radioed by Ground Control. They were vectored to Swanage, to intercept the leading formations of the Nazi raiders. But when they arrived there was nothing——not a "blip" on the screen, and beyond the canopy only solid, pitchy blackness. Cunningham circled, relaxed in his seat, eyes flicking over his instruments; waiting. Long nights of vigil had given him immense patience.

Empty minutes, then Control came through: "Bandit

in your area . . . Steer 0-2-5, angels nine." Cunningham
swung on to the bearing, climbed to nine thousand feet
and very soon picked up a faint " blip " dead ahead. He
closed up to just over 1,000 yards, and then suddenly the
" blip " began to move very rapidly across the radar
screen—the raider had turned about, and now was racing
back towards him ! In complete darkness, the two machines
were converging head-on, at an aggregate speed of over
500 miles an hour !

Seconds to think. Cunningham kept his Mahatma-calm,
his shoulders remained resting, relaxed, against the back of
his seat even as the enemy's streams of tracer came lobbing
towards them, passing so close that the Beaufighter bucked
and shuddered. He did not return the fire—it was not
John Cunningham's habit to blaze away wildly, he never
pressed the button until he had " everything lined up "
and was perfectly sure of hitting the target. Smoothly,
unhurriedly, it seemed—he banked the plane and went
into a tight, climbing turn.

As they rose out of the claws of the tracer, a slender,
barely discernible shadow flitted by underneath. " Heinkel,"
Rawnsley announced quietly. Cunningham wheeled round
after it, but it had vanished, his screen was blank. He
circled, called up Ground Control : " Standing by—up
to you again. . . ."

While they waited, hovering in the high dark, Cunningham reflected that the Germans' new radio device certainly
seemed effective—the Heinkel's captain had been warned
that a fighter was coming up behind him, perhaps even
informed of the pursuer's height and range. And this
business of turning back to meet the attacker, head-on,
was a new and bold procedure. All this might call for
new tactics, a fresh approach. . . .

Ground Control's plotters were not long in tracking down the Heinkel. It had turned north, towards Shaftesbury. A new course and height to fly—and Cunningham was back in the hunt.

He picked up the raider again only minutes later. And once more it wheeled on the instant to face him. Visibility was better here and for fleeting seconds he saw it clearly, charging at him. He kicked his rudder, slid neatly out of its path. Rushing past at close range the German raked the Beaufighter with its 'midship guns, and was gone.

Cunningham knew then that it was his rare—and doubtful—luck to be up against an ace bombing pilot. It is not often in modern war that two truly great pilots chance to oppose each other in personal battle. Cunningham, so far getting the worst of the duel, decided that his best chance lay in a " winding match "—a complicated, physically exacting and extremely hazardous manœuvre in which two aircraft try to out-turn each other. He checked the Beaufighter, could find no serious damage. If only he could tempt the German into this trap, he was confident he could get round inside him and thus bring his guns to bear on the tail. In the meantime he would save his ammo.

The Heinkel had straightened out and resumed its northerly course, cutting through rearing wads of cloud. Cunningham once more groped for him by radar, closed in from behind. For the third time the German started to wheel tightly, to hunt the hunter.

But the Englishman, ready for him this time, turned too, before the bomber could get round—banking the Beaufighter vertically, pirouetting tightly on his wingtip. So tightly it hurt : centrifugal force, like the hands of an invisible giant, pressed on the heads of pilot and navigator, slamming them down into their seats, turning their limbs to immovable lead, draining the blood supply from eye and brain until the instrument dials became blurred, meaningless splotches. When he judged they were round, heading back the way they had come, Cunningham took off some of the bank ; at once the pressure lifted, everything came back into focus. And now the roles were reversed, they had the Heinkel chasing them.

Cunningham continued to turn, but not too steeply now. Sure enough, the German followed him round. Cunningham advanced his throttles, little by little increased bank and rudder, gradually tightening up again. The Heinkel fell into his trap, tried to stay with him.

As once more the wings neared the vertical position several of the Beaufighter's most important instruments went mad, for the spinning gyroscopes that controlled them toppled at this angle. Beyond the windscreen darkened earth and overcast sky were merged in unbroken dimness —there was no faintest hint of a horizon for Cunningham to use as a reference, and as ten, twenty, thirty seconds strained by Rawnsley, slumped in the rear seat, lost all sense of direction, could not tell which way was up and which was down . . . But so skilled was Cunningham that, with only a few basic instruments still operating, he was able to hold the plane steady in its full-banked, full-powered circling. And somehow he managed to keep raising his head to search the darkness around them with those incredible, gloom-piercing eyes, trying to keep track of the Heinkel.

Forty seconds, fifty, sixty. . . . The crushing weight of the centrifugal force increased until Rawnsley could no longer hold his head up ; his chin went down, pressed against his chest, and the cabin seemed to fill with swirling, red mist. He wondered how his Skipper hoped to distinguish anything—even his instrument panel—under so much " G " stress.

Cunningham was fighting to stop himself " blacking out." His locked neck and jaw muscles ached and quivered under the strain, he was having trouble breathing —when he let the air out of his lungs they wanted to remain deflated, and it was hard labour to get them filled again. And even his remarkable vision was suffering as the blood drained from his cranium; thick black streaks of " rain " appeared, slashing down across windscreen and instrument panel. But he knew the bigger, less manœuvrable Heinkel could not turn as tightly as this, no matter how good the pilot. And he knew he must hold on or be trapped himself—he was committed now, to take off any of the bank would mean flying right into the enemy's sights !

The engines shrieked, the fighter began to vibrate violently, and all track of time was lost. Afterwards they could not be sure how long they had kept up the punishing " merry-go-round " before, very suddenly, the dark silhouette and glowing exhausts of the Heinkel materialised out of the darkness—very close, almost directly above the Beaufighter's canopy ! The fighter had turned in a smaller circle, come up behind the bomber.

Immediately Cunningham eased back his throttles, took off a little bank. The gruelling " G " pressure lessened. He let the enemy draw ahead a little, drew a deep breath and, cool and methodical as a butler setting a breakfast tray, adjusted his gun-sight and laid it on the Heinkel's tail.

But in that instant, just as his thumb took the first, light pressure on the firing button, the bomber flicked out of its steep turn, twisted away in the opposite direction then plummeted down in an almost sheer dive. Perhaps the

German pilot's physical endurance was at an end, or having lost all trace of the Beaufighter he decided to break off the engagement. Possibly his new radio device warned him that his adversary was once again on his tail and, just in time, he saw the trap he'd been drawn into.

Cunningham put the stick forward, dived after him. But beneath lay clouds thick as wool, with hilltops thrusting up into them. The high ground cluttered the Beaufighter's radar with huge shadows, making a crazy jigsaw of the screen and masking the " blip " of the fugitive bomber.

Rawnsley was snarling in angry disappointment but the " imperturbable Baby-Face " merely shrugged, climbed, set course for base.

Not until late the next day did the news reach Middle Wallop : the Heinkel had not escaped, it had crashed on a hilltop near Cranbourne Chase. In his desperate dive to shake off the Beaufighter the German had struck high ground hidden in the dense cloud. Intelligence had managed to identify the pilot as Hauptmann Langar, celebrated Luftwaffe ace and commander of the K.Gr 100 development unit.

Without firing a shot Cunningham had won his duel. By patience, daring tactics and sheer flying ability, he had vanquished a top pilot from a crack enemy unit. And he had proved that the Luftwaffe's new radio device could be beaten by resolute, resourceful defenders.

This single incident—so typical of Cunningham's war —had a profound effect on the future tactics of the entire R.A.F. night-fighter force.

John Cunningham attained the rank of Group Captain, and an official " bag " of twenty enemy aircraft. Men who flew with him declared that in fact he had destroyed at least another ten, but in the darkness and confusion of night operations it was often difficult, and sometimes impossible, to confirm " kills " and establish which pilots had made them.

From early childhood he had been familiar with, and deeply interested in, aeroplanes, for the family home was close by Croydon airport on the outskirts of London. It was natural that he should become an apprentice at the De Havilland Aeronautical Technical School, and later join the Auxiliary Air Force.

And it was natural that when peace was won, and he left the service, this cool-headed, outstanding airman with the scientific bent should become chief test pilot of Britain's proud new jetliner, the De Havilland Comet, and nurse that mighty plane through experimental stages, setbacks and crises, to record-breaking fame.

CHAPTER FOURTEEN

THE AMAZON HAS WINGS

THE DEEP, vengeful roar of the Russian artillery rolled through the smoky, rubbled streets of Berlin, a dying city. While Adolf Hitler crouched in his bunker—an elaborate, bomb-proof underground headquarters—less than a mile distant his personal suicide troops, the " Praetorian Guard " of the Third Reich, were making a fanatically brave stand against the powerful Soviet infantry formations pouring in from the outskirts, thrusting for the heart of the crumbling Nazi capital.

In the bunker, the din of the barrage and the street battles could not be heard. Closing his eyes and ears to the true grimness of the situation, Hitler studied his maps and explained to the small group of followers who remained his wild, last-hope plan to counter-attack, save the city and himself from the Allied fury. Then he dictated a curt message for his air commanders. Minutes later a diminutive figure in overalls and flying helmet slipped from the bunker into the thundery haze of the outside world.

Thirty-two-year-old Hanna Reitsch, one of the greatest women flyers of all time, carried from the surrounded bunker the most dramatic—and hopeless—S.O.S. of the war. Hitler had chosen her to pilot the last plane out of Berlin, and contact the Luftwaffe chiefs whom he believed were still operational outside the Soviet

ring which encircled him. "Only with aerial help,"
he had written, "can General Wenck's army relieve the
capital."

What the Fuhrer did not know—or refused to accept—
was that Wenck's army existed only on paper. Russian
ground and air attacks had long since smashed it to pieces.
And nearly all of the few, isolated Luftwaffe bases which
remained outside the range of the invading Allied armies
were under constant bombing and strafing attacks—it was
doubtful if any could have got more than two or three
planes into the air. Hour upon hour, shell and bombfire
marched down the runways, smashed the parked aircraft
like bugs, crumpled the hangars and control towers like
empty cigarette packets. Most squadrons were without
reserves of fuel and ammunition, and with the country's
main road and rail arteries cut or blocked there was prac-
tically no chance of fresh supplies reaching them. Communications were becoming chaotic and many commanders
had lost touch with each other, and with the general
picture—everywhere was confusion and the bitter stench
of defeat.

But the Fuhrer had said Wenck and the Luftwaffe would
save him—and Hanna Reitsch even now believed implicitly
every word he uttered. A tragically misplaced patriotism,
and a complete capacity for loyalty, long ago had made
this five-foot-tall, blonde aviatrix one of the Nazi dictator's
most passionate admirers and eager servants. In 1942
he had strengthened her pride and devotion by decorating
her with the Iron Cross (First Class)—after that there can
be no doubt that Hanna was as passionate a Nazi as any of
the others who served the swastika.

There can be no doubt, either, that she served heroically.
And in this book we are concerned mainly with heroism

in the air—the causes and motives involved are of secondary
interest.

Hanna's brilliance and bravery as a pilot had won her
many friends in England in 1937 when she arrived to take
part in the annual soaring competition held by the British
Gliding Association at Great Hucklow, Derbyshire. And
her endless efforts to encourage women everywhere to take
to the air and make careers for themselves in the growing
aircraft industries " on an equal basis with men " got a good
deal of publicity. She was then 24, and had been given the
rank of Captain by the German Air Ministry in recognition
of her work as a test pilot. Famed for her precision flying,
she had challenged top German airmen to contests involving
complicated patterns, instrument flying and aerobatics—
and more often than not been judged the victor. She spent
every hour she could in the air, and was familiar with
scores of aircraft types.

Hanna believed that British girls, like their German
" cousins," had certain " national qualities " which were
suited to flying. She was full of praise for Amy Johnson,
the English ex-typist who had been the first woman to fly
solo from London to Australia in 1930, and in 1931 had
set up a record by flying alone from England to India in
six days.

Amy was about ten years older than Hanna, and start-
lingly different in personality. The English girl had a
simple love of aeroplanes, a natural flying skill and a hard-
won, carefully husbanded store of aviation knowledge.
Her only purpose was to go on flying, and meeting all the
challenges it offered her, for as long as she could. Quiet-
spoken and completely unaffected—genuinely shy, many
thought—she was entirely without fierce national pride or

fashionable theories, and she saw herself as representative of no particular class or cause.

The British public held Amy in warm affection, and to this other girl pilot from abroad—dubbed, indeed, by some newspapers "Germany's Amy Johnson"—a special welcome was extended. Her coolness and outstanding skill in flying gliders through the tricky winds above the hills of Nottinghamshire and Derbyshire brought unstinted praise from air experts, and many leading British flyers entertained her in their homes.

Hanna was eager to recruit enthusiasts in Britain for her "equal rights for women in the air" campaign, and her idea about "national qualities"—which to some English minds had a strong reek of Nordic racial theories. She grew impatient when—despite her lavish tributes to Amy Johnson—none of her hosts seemed to take her schemes seriously. There is every indication that she returned to Germany convinced that Britain was "lackadaisical, backward, decadent"—everything that the Nazis said it was. And two years later, when war came, Captain Reitsch volunteered for flying duties "in an operational capacity." She even offered to form a special squadron of women pilots "to fight for the Fatherland, on the same terms as the men of the Luftwaffe—without any privileges or restrictions."

Nazi propaganda chief Joseph Goebbels saw in her a valuable property, and used her to symbolise the spirit of German womanhood at war—recruiting girls for ground duties with the Luftwaffe, for munitions factories and other forms of national service. She worked as test pilot for many of the latest fighters and bombers; flew Generals and high Nazi officials in and out of occupied countries and operational theatres (more than once having to run the gauntlet of enemy flak or fighters), acted as liaison officer flying between forward bases and headquarters, and for a time was Hitler's personal pilot. Often as she whisked him across Germany the dictator would ask her advice on aviation matters.

But her repeated requests to be allowed to form and train an all-woman squadron to fly on bomber or fighter operations were tactfully brushed aside. Hitler is said to have told her: " You are more valuable to me in your present duties."

Meanwhile Amy Johnson was also serving her country. She had no grand schemes about forming girl pilots into combat units, and no photographers or propagandists followed her around—as a ferry pilot with Air Transport Auxiliary she was busy flying new aircraft of all types, from fighters to the biggest bombers, from the factories to the R.A.F. bases where they were so urgently needed. All over the country and abroad she flew, by day or by night, often in foul weather.

On a grey day in 1941 a multi-engined plane she was ferrying over Southern England developed a series of faults. Amy fought coolly, using all her vast experience, but she lost control. Over the Thames Estuary she baled out, and was drowned.

In far-off Russia, where even before the war Communism had introduced a greater equality of the sexes, the story was different. In the tense summer of 1941 Marina Raskova, one of the most experienced Soviet airwomen, was checked out by Red Air Force instructors on every type of operational plane in service. She then called together from all areas of the vast Union, all the girls who held pilots' certificates and taught them to fly fighters and bombers.

First woman to hold the Air Force rank of Colonel, Marina got her government's approval of a scheme to form all-women squadrons for combat duties. She herself later took command of a " mixed " bomber squadron—eighty per cent of the air crews were female. Its record was as good as any in the service.

The girl fighter pilots were commanded by Lieutenant Colonel " Niki " Kezarinova, who held the Order of Lenin and the Red Star. Top ace of this " pursuit regiment " was Captain Lydia Litviak who, during the desperate air battles over besieged Stalingrad, destroyed twelve German machines. Lydia was killed during the Soviet offensive at Orel in 1943.

One of the strangest air operations of any war took place over German artillery fortifications at Krimskaya in June, 1943. It might be called " the battle of the Amazons."

Nine Russian dive-bombers, all crewed by women, were ordered to destroy the Nazi guns. They were escorted to the target by a wing of fighters, also flown by women and commanded by Captain A. Timofeyeva—mother of two children, who had worked before the war as a weaver.

Cloudy conditions forced them to approach the target dangerously low—at about 2,800 feet. As the dive-bombers dipped their noses and started to scream down through a thick curtain of A.A. fire, a pack of Messerschmitts swooped out of the cloud cover in a perfect " bounce " and tried to fasten on to their tails.

Captain Timofeyeva brought her fighters down after the Germans and the Nazi pilots were astonished to hear on their radios high, unmistakably female voices calling to each other ! Perhaps the surprise put them off their stride—at any rate, they failed to catch up with the dive-bombers, or to make them break off their attack.

The Soviet bombs erupted in and all around the German battery—and then the dive-bombers, instead of fleeing across country, keeping very low and slewing from side to side to shake off the Messerschmitts, suddenly formed up and wheeled in a neat, pre-arranged manœuvre to face their attackers. Their turn was right—the faster, less manœuvrable Messerschmitts could not get round in such a small circle, but were lured into trying. The German pilots found themselves caught in a deadly crossfire —between the dive-bombers and the escorting fighters.

In a matter of seconds four of the German planes were shot down. The rest broke formation, turning and climbing and diving—heading off in each and every direction to get out of the crossfire. The Red Amazons, with the sky to themselves, turned in orderly formation for home. Three of the dive-bombers were damaged and one, piloted by Maria Dolyena, had flames trailing from the rear fuselage. But all made it back to base.

Intelligence reports of such encounters with Soviet women pilots were kept secret in Berlin, but the news reached Hanna Reitsch. Again she asked permission to train German women pilots for combat, but again she was refused—it was too late, the Allied invasions, and the round-the-clock bomber offensive were cutting production, and it was a big enough problem to keep present squadrons supplied with replacement aircraft.

So Hanna had to content herself with the various assignments Hitler chose to give her. And the last of them was that dramatic S.O.S. from the Berlin bunker, on that April night in 1945.

An armoured vehicle was waiting to take her to Brandenburger Tor, where her Arado 96 was hidden in a special shelter. Accompanying her was General von Greim—pale, hollow-eyed, wordless.

They clambered into the vehicle and Hanna sat beside the driver,—a young, poker-faced S.S. volunteer; von Greim hunched down in the back, consumed with his private miseries. They started off, lurching crazily over hunks of masonry and piles of debris. In the distance now huge fires were raging, washing the night sky with a fierce crimson. Salvoes of shells screamed down, crashed into buildings all around, showered the vehicle with fragments of stone and shrapnel.

Each time they heard the screaming of falling shells, the driver swerved out into the middle of the littered roadway, so that if a building on either side were hit there would be less chance of the vehicle being completely buried by the falling wreckage. And he avoided the narrower streets.

Hanna began to worry that her secret plane-shelter was already in Russian hands. " Faster ! " she yelled, above the storm of the battle. " Forget about swerving—take the shortest route ! "

They were within a quarter of a mile of the Arado's hiding place when a salvo smashed into the roadway so close behind them that the armoured vehicle was lifted into the air, carried sideways by the blast, and dumped down again with tremendous force. It staggered on for a few yards, rocking wildly, then snarled to a halt. The driver, blood running down his face from where he had struck it against a stanchion, could not get it moving again.

Hanna wheeled, shook von Greim's drooping shoulder, then climbed out. The street was full of hot drifting dust and smoke and the sinister, flickering light from a thousand burning buildings. Ducking round shell-holes, scrambling over the rubble, together they half-ran, half-crawled the rest of the way to the plane-shelter. The Arado was undamaged.

While they worked to prepare for the take-off, crouched figures flitted past the end of the broad avenue outside. Machine-guns rasped, rifles barked and whined, grenades crumped, there were hoarse cries and shrill whistles—they knew they were on the very fringe of the street fighting.

Hanna taxied out, pointed the Arado's nose up the dark, smoky roadway which was to be her runway. For all she knew there might be a yawning crater dead ahead, or a barricade of masonry, but there was no time to check. She glanced at von Greim—deathly pale, staring fixedly ahead with those hollow eyes. Then she advanced the throttle and the little craft started to roll.

Just after the tail came up one wheel struck a big stone. The Arado tilted, swung round, one wingtip scraping the ground. Hanna saw the dark bulk of a shattered building looming ahead and knew she had to take a chance and try to haul the plane off before it had built up a safe margin of speed. Both hands on the stick : the plane was reluctant to rise, but came up mushily, wings juddering and dipping, a hair's breadth above stalling point. Hanna fought it round slowly, with the minimum of bank, away from the shattered building. Then she let the nose down a shade, kept going straight on up the avenue, with the wheels scant inches from the littered surface, and held it there until at last she had built up climbing speed.

As they rose above the rooftops into a dark red sky the full, appalling vista was revealed—a great city burning, breaking up, perishing under their wings. Great columns crashed in plumes of sparks, ancient structures blazed like lanterns, exploding shells flashed in expanding rings, and over all the long, glowing spears of tracer stitched a criss-cross pattern, like a vast golden net.

And then the searchlights hit her. Searing, pounding, blinding light—a Russian battery on the outskirts swung all its beams on to the little Arado, held it in a cone while scores of heavy machine-guns and light A.A. pieces clawed for it.

Hanna threw the plane violently from side to side, climbed, dived, side-slipped. Still the vice of beams gripped her, and the blast of the flak made the controls kick furiously in her hands.

" I'm going down ! " she bawled to von Greim, but he stared blankly, apparently not understanding her. She cut the throttle, slammed the stick forward. The Arado plummeted, almost vertically, back into the smoke over the dying city.

The searchlights tried to follow but Hanna did not pull out until she was skimming over the shattered rooftops. Having shaken them off, she stayed at this height—now and then having to tweak a wing up over a broken factory chimney, or a fractured church spire—until they were clear of the suburbs. It was a superb, courageous example of evasive action, of which any experienced combat pilot could have been proud. And it was done in the most dangerous conditions—at night, with drifting smoke and dust obscuring the windscreen at times, and obstacles materialising suddenly out of the gloom.

Reaching open country she climbed to 20,000 feet and set course for the fifty-minute flight to Rechlin, still in German hands and headquarters of a Luftwaffe group.

She knew the worst was still to come—the sky all

around the city was alive with Russian fighters. Convinced
that Hitler and the other Nazi leaders would make a last-
minute bid to fly out to Switzerland, Sweden or some other
neutral country, the Red Air Force had built a thick, high
wall of patrols around the city and the pilots had orders
to let no plane pass, whatever its type or markings.

Luckily there were occasional clumps of cloud. She
made her way from one to another, twisting her neck to
search the sky all around as she skipped across the clear
patches. Several times, high above or off to one side, she
saw groups of Soviet fighters silhouetted against the stars
or the red glow of the burning city, and they failed to spot
her. But such luck could not last. . . .

Four of them. Slanting down from behind, coming very
fast in loose, line-abreast formation, the leading edges of
their wings barbed with wicked little spikes of blue and
red flame, flickering fiercely, as they fired long bursts.
Hanna stood the Arado on a wingtip, hauled it round,
dived hard. The fighters followed, but could not turn as
tightly. She pulled up again, into the sanctuary of a cloud
and lost them. Only then did she discover that the Arado
had been hit. Pieces had been chivvied out of the tail
assembly and the rear fuselage, but the little craft still
responded perfectly to the controls.

She could see the sweat glistening on von Greim's white,
misery-broken face. She realised the man was resigned to
death, any minute now—he did not believe they had the
slightest chance of getting through to Rechlin. But Hanna,
aglow with the fire of the fanatic, had the feeling that she
held history in her hands ; she really believed the message
from the Fuhrer which she carried could save the Fatherland even now from the hated Bolsheviks. Emerging from
the cloud she settled down to fly as never before, putting

her neck into swivel-gear, scanning every corner of the night sky; with her reflexes poised, yet relaxed, her mind highly charged, yet unflustered—remembering even now to check the compass, altimeter, air speed indicator and all the other instruments with regular, swift, custom-learned flicks of the eyes, and managing to keep track of their progress towards Rechlin.

After about two minutes in the clear, two more fighters sliced down, this time almost dead ahead. As they came, they slid apart—to get on either side of her, so that when they opened up they could bring a crossfire to bear. But the watchful, sharp-sighted Hanna spotted them long before they were in range. And a bare instant before their guns blazed she put the Arado into a steep dive, dropped like a gannet for about 2,000 feet, then levelled out, banked steeply and cartwheeled to the right. This rapid, complex manœuvring shook off one of her attackers, but the other had dropped below and was now climbing under her belly, firing short bursts. His bullets drummed on the underside of the port wing, and a piece of the trailing edge fell off.

Hanna threw the nimble machine into a long, violent series of rolls and stalled turns, vertical dives and climbs, bunts and controlled spins, writhing about the sky like a maddened salmon fighting on the hook. She finished up right down on the deck, streaking across fields and villages so low that the plane's shape seemed to merge with the shadows of hills and valleys and pine thickets. She managed to lose the remaining fighter, but soon machine-guns on the ground opened up, and she was forced to climb again.

Now the Russians knew that a plane had got out of Berlin, and was trying to sneak through their blockade. Hanna reckoned that by now they must have realised she was heading for Rechlin—so all their fighters would be concentrated rapidly in this sector, and all ground defences would be warned. To make their tracking more difficult, she began to weave from side to side.

This time she didn't see them coming, the first she knew about it was when tracer flicked close by the cabin. The angle and density of the tracer told her there were at least two, diving from port in a beam attack. She rolled on her left side, turned in to face them—thereby altering the closing angle, shortening the time she would be in the line of fire, and presenting a smaller target. The first of them flashed by close overhead. The second hurtled towards her, head-on now, but he could not reduce his initial angle of deflection in time to get his fire on to her before he was forced to put his nose down and pass just underneath.

The instant both were behind her, Hanna wheeled again, raced after them at full throttle—gambling that this would be the very last thing they would expect. The gamble came off; the Red pilots, taking it for granted that she would be trying to put as much sky as possible between her and her pursuers, turned about and sped off in that direction. She saw them pass underneath. Seconds later she was plunging into a timely wad of cumulo-stratus.

She stayed in the cloud for two or three minutes, circling, then edged out and, scanning the faint grey-and-black pattern of the land below, managed to get her bearings. Her pulse quickened—she was almost through, another ten minutes would take her to Rechlin! And in that direction the clouds were thicker! She gave von Greim an encouraging grin, but he only nodded vaguely, stared about him with those deep, glazed eyes.

On that last stage of the nightmare flight Hanna spotted several more fighters—once a huge pack of them passed within two thousand yards, without sighting her. There was one more attack by a single Russian but there was a lot more cloud now and she managed to bury herself in it before he could get in a well-aimed burst. Then she was through the gauntlet. She dropped out of the overcast, made her landing approach a little faster than usual to allow for the damage to tail and rudder, touched down with the wheels first and taxied at high speed to the control tower, swerving round bomb craters and wrecked planes. As she cut the engine, von Greim looked as if he could not believe they were safely down. He remained perfectly still, blinking uncertainly; she had to shake him hard before he came to life, undid his straps and climbed out.

To the few haggard, listless senior officers of the Luftwaffe gathered at this base, Hanna formally delivered the Fuhrer's message, and General von Greim mustered enough concentration to issue orders calling every available German aircraft to the defence of Berlin. The General was not very convincing; it was plain he had no faith in his own words.

The Luftwaffe officers listened in silence, then explained politely that the small number of aircraft they could get airborne would be completely ineffective against the Soviet might. They had no replacements or spare parts, fuel and ammunition were almost exhausted. And besides, nearly all of them—like von Greim—saw that defeat was inevitable and were loath to send their surviving pilots, mostly very young recruits, on a suicide mission which could gain nothing.

Not so Hanna—furious at their " disloyalty," she persuaded von Greim to fly off with her to Ploen, near Keil, to see Grand Admiral Karl Doenitz, who was earmarked to become Nazi Supreme Commander if Hitler should be killed or captured. Her idea was that Doenitz, planner of the pitiless U-boat war and notorious " strong man " in past crises, would very quickly crack down on these Luftwaffe " shirkers," rally them—and the country—for a final effort.

Ploen was well out of the way of the Russians, and British and American aircraft in that area showed no interest in the light machine, so the flight was uneventful. So was the interview with Doenitz—he seemed suddenly to have aged ; her words clearly did not impinge on his consciousness. It was plain that he was preoccupied with the problems of food distribution, public health and essential services in the foundering Reich, all of which Hanna considered unimportant compared with the need to save Berlin and the Fuhrer.

Refusing to give up, and still dragging the dazed and depressed von Greim with her, Hanna sought out Field-Marshal Wilhelm Keitel, head of the Supreme Command—of which Hitler himself was the Commander-in-Chief. Keitel, his face deep-scored, his eyes bright-glazed as painted porcelain, listened to her passionate plea, that, even without air support, Wenck's army should move at once to the relief of Berlin. Then the man who, in just a few more days, was to sign an act of military surrender—and who eventually was to be condemned by an Allied tribunal and hanged as a war criminal—said very quietly and flatly : " Wenck's army has been destroyed. It is all over."

It was the tragic end of Hanna's hopeless mission. Her flight out of Berlin had been an epic—perhaps the most difficult and dangerous ever undertaken by a non-military flyer in an unarmed plane. Months later, Allied air experts piecing together the facts were forced to acknowledge her immense skill and heroism. Many expressed deep sadness that this outstanding woman pilot should have squandered

(*above*) A B-25 bomber takes off from the flight deck of the U.S. aircraft carrier *Hornet* for a raid on Japan.

(*below*) The U.S. base at Pearl Harbour after the Japanese attack. On the left is the light cruiser U.S.S. *Helena*, which although badly damaged, struck back with anti-aircraft guns and brought down six Japanese planes.

(*Photos: Imperial War Museum.*)

(*above*) Avro Lancasters, famous British heavy bombers, setting out for a heavy night raid on a German city. (*Photo: Maurice Allward.*)

(*below*) A U-boat caught in a hail of fire from a Sunderland flying-boat. (*Photo: Imperial War Museum.*)

her talents and loyalties in such a vicious cause. Some even sought to find excuses for her Nazi activities.

But Hanna Reitsch remained a faithful and defiant Nazi, even after news reached Ploen that Hitler and Eva Braun had died in the Berlin bunker, and that Russia's hammer-and-sickle flag was flying over the ruins of the capital.

On 2nd May, when a new German Government was convened at Ploen, she marched into the office of Heinrich Himmler, head of the Gestapo and now home front commander (who later committed suicide).

" Is it true" she demanded, " that you have contacted the Anglo-Americans with peace proposals ? "

" Of course," he said curtly. " There is nothing else to do now." Members of Himmler's staff and other officials and officers turned nervous glances on Hanna.

The five-foot Amazon stared into the hard eyes of the most feared man in Germany—the systematic killer who had ordered the deaths of countless thousands, from nameless concentration camp victims to powerful officials and top-ranking military officers. Her lips curled in contempt.

" Traitor ! " she shrilled. " You have betrayed your Fuhrer, and your people, in the very darkest hour." Then, blonde head high, she turned and marched from the room— soon to face Allied investigators, and pay the price for her misplaced devotion ; for the wasted years which, but for Adolf Hitler and his base creed, could have brought her fame and friendship throughout the world.

CHAPTER FIFTEEN

CANNON IN THE SKY

OVER THE quiet English countryside came two great
shuddering bangs, in quick succession, like the expanding
shock waves of a distant, mighty explosion. Workers in
the fields of Surrey felt a soft jolt in the air; flocks of
birds rose in whirring fright from the treetops, and in
farmsteads, hamlets and townships window-panes rattled
in their frames.

Everywhere people paused, peered skyward. A few
spotted a small, glinting fighter-plane streaking overhead,
but there was no reason to associate it with the mysterious
bangs—it was flying serenely, trailing no smoke. And
besides, aircraft like this were often seen over this part of
England nowadays; any schoolboy could identify those
swept-back wings—the new DH 108, experimental jet,
also known as the Swallow.

But they were wrong to dismiss the little plane as the
possible source of the big "explosion." For beneath the
Swallow's streamlined canopy was Squadron Leader John
Derry, one of the most brilliant and venturesome of that
small band of former war-flyers who, turning from bombs
and bullets to blueprints and prototype testing, were
piloting Britain to peace-time progress. And Derry had
just made history; that deep, shuddering noise rolling
over the countryside and echoing in the hills was, in one
sense, an explosion—Man's crashing of the Sound Barrier,
his bursting through into the Supersonic Age.

The time was 10.30 on a Monday morning in the Autumn of 1948 ; the place, an undefined area of the sky between ancient, royal Windsor and Farnborough, home of the Royal Aircraft Establishment and the showplace of modern aviation. By putting the Swallow into a flat-out power-dive from more than 30,000 feet, Derry had become the first human to fly faster than the speed of sound. And as the machine had caught up with the noise of its own passage through the air, there occurred that awesome phenomenon which was soon to become known as " the sonic boom," like two quick blasts from a mighty cannon, rolling across the sky and the land.

In those instants, going through the barrier, the Swallow had been subjected to savage buffeting. The sound waves cramming the air all around it set up a vibration that threatened to shake it to pieces. But Derry, and the creators of this new flying machine, had been well-prepared for this danger ; other pilots had drawn close to the barrier before, and been battered back. One, Captain Geoffrey De Havilland, distinguished military airman and member of the pioneer family which had founded the great De Havilland Aircraft Company, had lost his life only two years earlier, when his plane broke up in a barrier-piercing bid over the Thames Estuary.

Throughout history, the latent power of sound to produce destructive vibrations had been known. There was a clear enough warning in the Old Testament account of Joshua's trumpet razing the walls of Jericho, another in the story of Enrico Caruso, the superb Italian opera singer, shattering wine glasses with his powerful tenor voice !

Derry and his colleagues were sure that the answer was to smash through the barrier quickly—" like a dog jumping through a paper hoop." On the other side, once the juddering jumble of sound-waves had been left behind, they believed there lay an unknown world of safe, smooth silence; a world which must be reached and opened up for the great jet craft of the future.

Up till now no plane had been fast enough to break through quickly and cleanly, thereby being subjected only to a short, sharp " bump " of turbulence; but in the new, powerful, swept-wing Swallow they were confident they had the key which would open the way.

At sea level the speed of sound is approximately 760 m.p.h. But it decreases with altitude and with reduction in the density of the atmosphere, so to indicate this variable factor airmen use the term " Mach Number One." Whatever the height of the plane, whatever the *actual* speed of sound there, it is called " Mach 1."

To get a mental picture of this mysterious thing known as the Sonic Barrier, we first must understand that in front of an aircraft's wings as it proceeds through the air there is a kind of faint, restless stirring. Little waves of suction and pressure are continuously advancing ahead of the plane, probing forward, like long-range scouts—as though to warn the air of what is coming and start it flowing into submissive pattern before the machine itself arrives. Let us call this process " the run-ahead."

Now, the slower the plane is moving, the further the " run-ahead " will extend. Thus, long before the slow plane arrives, the sky is beginning to prepare itself, shaping its molecules and currents to accept the approaching wings. Few pilots can explain *why* the sky does this, but many see the phenomenon as startling proof that Man was meant to fly—" that the sky was designed to accept machines."

In faster aircraft, flying at around 600 m.p.h., the " run-ahead " extends only a little way forward—the plane is very nearly keeping up with its sound. And in an aircraft travelling at Mach 1—the varying speed of actual sound—the run-ahead stops entirely, and the " bow-wave " of air, unable to outspeed the machine, remains attached to wings and fuselage, building up with terrifying rapidity into a storm of shock-waves, buffeting and battering and threatening to break the plane in pieces.

To ride such a storm, even for a few instants, a special sort of wing design is needed ; a wing which not only can withstand the wild vibration of passing through the barrier, but which can also ride the still, " unwarned " sky beyond—ram into an atmosphere which has not been made aware of the machine's approach, and by sheer power and strength and delicacy of shape and balance fly smoothly on through air which has not had time to prepare itself for the plane's passage.

And as wings like these crash through the barrier, people on the ground usually hear not one, but two bangs. The second, of course, is an echo thrown back by the land. (Sometimes, in hilly districts, there are three " explosions," growing progressively fainter. But whatever the number of echoes, the occurrence is generally referred to in the singular, as " the sonic boom.")

For Derry, in his all-out dive, it came at 605.23 m.p.h. He felt a brief, brutal buffeting that had the controls kicking, bucking under his hands and feet, and he had to strain every muscle to hold the plane's nose down and the wings straight. And then—with incredible suddenness—he was through, the Swallow was flying smoothly downward through tranquil air ; he knew he was the first man into unknown territory, and he wondered at the deep, deep quietness, realised in a flash that jets of the future would travel in a soundless, pacific element, where the whine of motors and even the moan and hiss of wings cutting through the sky would be swept behind too fast to reach the ears of the occupants.

Then it was time to close the throttle, to ease back the stick—gently, smoothly!—and back out quickly, cleanly, through the breach he had made in the invisible wall. The turbulence this time was considerably less troublesome. In no time at all he was flying straight and level through the soft September sunlight, scudding across Surrey at about 500 m.p.h. towards Farnborough airfield. The Swallow was behaving normally, his body felt no different—oh, it was hard to believe he had been through the barrier, through to the silent world. . . !

A few hours later the Ministry of Supply released the bald, almost meaningless statement: "In the course of recent high speed development trials on the De Havilland 108 research aircraft, an apparent Mach number in excess of 1 was recorded." The people of Surrey heard this on the radio news, but still didn't connect it with the mysterious "explosion"—until the national Press explained, under huge headlines and blown-up portraits of John Derry, that a vital voyage of discovery had been successfully completed.

Derry's only comment to clamouring reporters was: "I cannot say I felt calm. . . . My tummy was full of butterflies." This was typical of the tall, modest, slow-speaking family man, the pilot who hated publicity. "Don't waste time on me," he would tell newsmen. "Go and talk to the men with the brains—the chaps who designed this kite, and planned the whole operation. . . ."

When war came in 1939, John Derry had been a 17-

year-old boarder at Charterhouse, one of Britian's most famous public schools. Adventure pulsed in his veins —his father, a doctor, had been a member of an archaeological expedition to Egypt's " Valley of the Kings " at Luxor. There was no hesitation in his choice—he volunteered for flying duties with the R.A.F. The pilot training schools were full ; he was happy to be accepted as a wireless-operator/air-gunner. Qualifying with high marks, he served with Coastal Command, won his commission and in time was appointed gunnery leader of his Group.

But the thrill of flying enchanted him and after a while being a mere crew-member—" a passenger "—was not enough ; he kept on applying for training as a pilot. Not until 1943 was he accepted and sent to a flying school in Canada.

He sailed through the course, without difficulty of any kind—he knew aeroplanes, he loved them, he understood the whole business of military aviation better than some of his instructors. Graduating with high ratings, he returned to Europe in time to serve in post-invasion operations. He won the D.F.C. " for great courage," and was also awarded the Bronze Lion of the Netherlands. His commanders reported that he had the simple but most valuable qualities —determination, and painstaking skill.

After the war there was no question about what career he would follow. His heart was in flying still, and the glowing reports in his log-book won him a post as test pilot with the Vickers-Armstrong company. In 1947, he moved to the De Havilland stable. With the DH experimental jets he smashed record after record, culminating in the Swallow's faster-than-sound flight in 1948.

Many more years might have passed before the sound barrier was pierced, and the honour might have gone to a pilot in another country had it not been for the genius and selfless, lifelong labour of an older airman—Group Captain Frank Whittle, " father of the jet engine." He was one of the " men with brains " that Derry so often praised, that rare combination of aeronautical scientist and active aviator.

As a lad of fifteen, Whittle had applied to enter the R.A.F as an apprentice. He was turned down. His rejection report said simply : " Poor physique." And there was no arguing —Frank was barely five feet tall, and very thin. Bitterly disappointed and very ashamed, he went to a physical training establishment, asked to see the chief instructor and explained his problem. The instructor, wholly sympathetic, gave the boy a list of body-building exercises and directions for a weight-increasing diet, the basis of which was olive oil.

In less than six months Frank's chest had expanded three inches and he'd gained nearly four in height. Once more he applied to the R.A.F. And once more he was refused. The air force doctors said he was still too skinny and muscularly weak.

Frank came home, went through the whole diet and exercise procedure again, from the very start. Then he applied for the third time—in another town, not mentioning his previous, unsuccessful applications. He passed all the tests, at last was accepted as a boy apprentice and posted to the R.A.F's Cranwell College.

Accepted for pilot training, the future jet pioneer made his first solo flight in an Avro 504N biplane, which had a top speed of 105 m.p.h.

In the midst of all this, at the age of 21, while still a cadet, he wrote a science thesis in which he discussed a new, revolutionary type of aircraft which would be propelled " by ejected gases." The existing system of piston engines and propellors was, he believed, decidedly limited; even with improved design and development such aircraft could not be expected to exceed speeds beyond 400 m.p.h.

That thesis was, in fact, the world's first clear exposition on the subject of jet flight. It won Whittle the college's highest award for aeronautical sciences.

So outstanding was his flying ability that on graduating he was made first an instructor, and later a test pilot on seaplanes. He devoted his spare time to designing the first jet engine, and in January, 1930, took out a master patent, submitted his drawings to the Air Ministry. The idea was rejected—" because the practical difficulties are too great."

After unsuccessful attempts to interest commercial firms, early in 1935 he formed a partnership with two other R.A.F. men and registered a company, Power Jets Ltd. Shown further designs, the Air Ministry experts now conceded that the basic principles were sound, but they still believed that the idea lay too far in the future. There appeared to be ample justification for this assessment, for the first engines which the company produced failed completely.

Whittle had put his all into the venture. Only a deep faith in his theory, and the same unflagging determination which years before had got him into the air force, kept him going now in his small workshop at Rugby. Through all the days of 1936 nothing but misfortune seemed to come his way. Friends advised him to give up the whole project, to concentrate on being an airman and leave engineering and invention to the great factories with unlimited funds and huge research staffs. Then in April, 1937, one of the Whittle jet engines ran properly for the first time. Scientists and flying men rushed to see a demonstration and were deeply impressed. There was champagne that night, and Frank kept one of the bottles—with forty signatures on its label.

But still he got no official backing. While the shadows of crisis were deepening in Europe, and in other lands air-minded governments were ordering their aircraft designers to begin experiments with a view to producing jet-propelled fighters, the little workshop at Rugby remained silent. Whittle wrote letters, sought interviews in Whitehall, constantly campaigning for an earnest development programme, pointing out that Britain was losing the chance of leading the world into the Jet Age. Not until early 1939—a few months before the outbreak of war—did he receive an order to build an engine which could be used to power a new, specially designed plane.

The job went ahead in strictest secrecy. Whittle worked with demoniac energy, depriving himself of sleep and proper meals, rushing back and forwards between Whitehall, Rugby and the various factories and experimental airfields where the makers of the airframe were conducting tests.

One of the biggest problems in this period was fuel consumption. The jet engine promised to give fantastic speed and rate of climb, but it burned fuel so quickly that the plane would be able to stay in the air only for a few minutes. There were many bitter setbacks before a means was found to make the engine run more economically and to provide additional fuel storage space in the wings and fuselage.

All through the tense Summer and Autumn of 1940, and the first winter of *blitzkrieg* bombing, while the young pilots of the R.A.F. fought by day and by night to defend a sorely beleaguered Britain, the older pilot, Frank Whittle, fought a different sort of round-the-clock battle, on the ground. And on a fine May morning in 1941, all the years of patience and toil were rewarded when a strange, propellerless machine whined across the Home Counties, sending people running to their air-raid shelters—convinced that this was some Nazi secret weapon, a giant bomb with wings.

He had got the first jet aircraft into the sky. The Whittle power unit drove it at a speed which exceeded his highest hopes: fully 200 m.p.h. faster than the swiftest piston-engined fighter of the day!

An intensive programme of tests and modification followed. Many improvements were made in both engine and airframe design, and the plane's endurance was increased still further. As the Gloster Meteor, it went into production for the R.A.F.

The first Meteors saw action in 1944. Their first great success was against the V.1 robot bombs, which were too fast for Fighter Command's ordinary, piston-engined planes.

A famous American pilot, General " Hap " Arnold, had seen some of the early tests with the experimental Gloster jet, powered by the Whittle-1 jet unit. He expressed amazement when he learned that this engine weighed only 650 pounds and provided more thrust than a comparable Rolls-Royce reciprocating engine weighing 1,650 pounds, and had only one-fifth the number of moving parts. It was easier to build and service, and would run on alcohol, diesel oil or paraffin.

Now, as a result of Arnold's report and the success of the service Meteor, United States manufacturers took up Whittle's invention and invited him to Washington to supervise the launching of an immense development and construction plan. But the years of feverish work and unrelenting strain were taking toll of his slight frame ; his health broke, he had to retire for long spells of hospital treatment. One of the most important periods of development in the history of aviation went ahead without him.

In June, 1946, pronounced fit again, he handed over to the British government all his interests in Power Jets Ltd., without asking a penny. By this act, he gave his life's work to the nation. Into the British Treasury, America poured millions of badly needed dollars in royalties on Whittle's patents.

He accepted the exacting and responsible post of planning and creating his country's future, all-jet air force. And the man whom many now regarded as the greatest air inventor since the Wright Brothers was content to live quietly in a small, rented house on an income of about £2,000 a year.

But the authorities had no intention of letting his genius and devotion go unrewarded. One day a courier knocked at the door of his little house, handed over a letter from the Royal Commission on Awards to Inventors. It told him he had been granted the sum of £100,000—the highest award Britain had ever made to an inventor.

And in 1948 came another, different sort of reward for " the father of the jet engine "—the news that 26-year-old John Derry had broken through the sound barrier. It was the realisation of Whittle's most precious dream. The way was now open, a bridgehead had been established in the supersonic stratosphere : soon great jetliners would soar in silence, without even noticeable vibration in their pressurised passenger cabins, into a new age of air travel.

In 1949 and 1950, the people of the Home Counties grew accustomed to the deep, double clap of " the sonic boom," as—almost daily, it seemed—Derry and his colleagues continued to thrust through the barrier with newer, ever-faster jets. Sometimes the shock-waves shattered windows or greenhouses : then there would be claims for damages, angry letters to the newspapers. All just claims got sympathetic consideration—it was a small price to pay for mastery of the supersonic sky. . . .

In France, Jacqueline Auriol, daughter-in-law of the President, soon became the first woman to fly faster than sound. Again and again she cracked the barrier, and won recognition as one of the world's greatest Jet Age test pilots.

In 1954, Jacqueline crashed on the River Seine, near Paris, and was gravely injured. Doctors feared her flying career was finished, but with great courage and tenacity she went through a difficult rehabilitation course and less than two years later was back at the controls.

And on 26th August, 1959, Madame Auriol—mother of two children—flew France's new delta-winged Mirage Mark III interceptor at 1,345 m.p.h.—*twice* the velocity of sound, the fastest speed ever achieved by a woman.

In Britain, from 1950 onwards, strangely-shaped, still-secret jet machines began to dominate each annual Farnborough Air Show. In 1952, the greatest attraction there was the brand-new, super-priority DH 110 fighter, to be piloted by the conqueror of the sound barrier, John Derry.

The vast, neck-craning crowd stirred in excitement, television and film cameras swung on to the slender, grey, twin-boomed craft as Derry climbed on board, took off and—with ridiculous ease—climbed almost vertically. The 110 dwindled to a speck . . . vanished from view. And all in a matter of seconds.

Eight miles up, Derry wheeled, put the nose down—

pointing straight at the tiny patch which was the airfield—
and began his barrier-piercing dive. His intention was to
pull out and sweep over the Farnborough crowd, fairly
low, at a speed considerably greater than Mach 1.

Bang-bang—far below the crowd heard the familiar double-
boom—the impact of the plane going through the barrier,
closely followed by an echo from the ground. And then
came a third bang. . . .

An instant later the DH 110 came hurtling out of the blue
distance, trying to pull out of its dive. Thousands of eyes
widened in horror as they saw pieces tearing away from
the fuselage!

Derry made a gallant bid to get clear of the airfield. The
plane was coming apart in his hands, yet somehow he
managed to pull the nose up, haul her into almost level
flight. The 120,000 spectators huddled close together and
the show's commentator yelled, " Look out, look out ! "
over the dozens of loudspeakers as the jet streaked overhead, breaking up as it went. For a moment it looked as if
the pilot's superhuman effort would succeed, that he would
manage to take his machine and himself to die in open
country beyond the airfield. But the 110 gave a sudden
lurch, went into a roll.

And disintegrated.

Jagged pieces of metal sprayed the spectators. One of
the engines sailed in a great glowing arc and, pitiless as a
flensing knife, ripped a long hole through a section of
the crowd on a hillock. Part of a wing slammed down
on the runway. The shattered tail assembly and the
mangled cockpit section spiralled slowly down after all the
rest.

Eighteen spectators died, many more were injured. The
body of John Derry lay not far from them, on a bank of

grass. It was four years to the day since he had broken through the sound barrier for the first time.

And as the ambulances raced out to collect the injured, the show commentator's voice came again over the loudspeakers. " This is one of the tragic risks of high speed research," he said, " but the work must go on."

Mere minutes later Squadron Leader Neville Duke, another famous British pilot and a close friend of John Derry, took his Hawker Hunter jet up to 40,000 feet and brought it down in a great, glinting dive.

Bang-bang.

CHAPTER SIXTEEN

WINGS OF MERCY

" GEIGER ? OH, thank Heaven—look, there's been an accident on Monte Rosa ! A climber's fallen on the rock face up by the summit—they've found him, but he's in a bad way."

Hermann Geiger half-turned, peered out of his window ; all grim and grey and dangerous out there, with the slow, slanting sleet blurring out the streets of the little Swiss town of Sion.

" I'm sorry," Geiger said. " I can't possibly, fly in this weather."

" But you *must* come—the search party say if this man isn't in hospital within a few hours he'll die for sure ! To bring him down by stretcher, in these conditions, would take the best part of a day. . . . Hallo, you still there ? "

" Yes, I'm here." Geiger was thinking, arguing with himself—the sane part of him was saying it was suicide to go near the peaks to-day, but the other part, the part that understood the misery and agony of an injured man lying up there in the thin, bone-chilling air, was insisting that he had no right to abandon this unknown climber without at least giving it a try. . . .

" All right," he said after a few seconds, " I'll have a shot at it. But I don't think there's much hope."

The thick cloud made a leaden roof over the whole Rhône Valley at just five hundred feet, and beneath it the

(*above*) Hermann Geiger (right) making a rescue in the Swiss Alps with his Piper Cub aircraft. (*Photo: Maurice Allward.*)

(*below*) The De Havilland D.H.110 which exploded in mid-air at the 1952 Farnborough Air Display, killing its test pilot John Derry (inset). (*Photo: Keystone Press Agency.*)

"The Fastest Man on Earth."

(*above*) Dr. John P. Stapp stands by the rocket sled in which he rode at a speed of 421 m.p.h. The sled consists of two vehicles; a propulsion unit driven by up to twelve 4,500 lb. thrust rockets, and a test vehicle weighing 2,000 lbs.

(*below*) This picture was taken an instant after 27,000 lbs. of rocket thrust started Dr. Stapp on the fastest ride man has taken on the ground.

(Photos: U.S. Information Service.)

sleet reduced visibility to less than a hundred yards as the single-engined Piper Cub, light and small as a toy, took off and headed unsteadily in the direction of the rearing mass of snow, ice and granite which is Europe's mightiest mountain bastion—the Alps. Once again the veteran pilot of the peaks was " giving it a try."

In his early forties, sturdily built and permanently tanned, Geiger had one of the most unusual and dangerous flying jobs in the world. His chief task was to supply food, fuel, medical kits and blankets to the scores of mountaineering huts and shelters which are scattered throughout the high Alps—resting places and refuges for skiers and climbers. In an hour he could complete a " round " which would take a string of pack-mules and drivers several days.

In addition, in the winter months he frequently flew food, medicine or special equipment to remote villages and lodges cut off by drifts or avalanches. Day by day he kept an eye on particularly heavy drifts building up above the passes, gave warning of areas where avalanches were likely. And when a big climbing party was making an assault on the great-fanged Matterhorn, he would check their progress every few hours and report to friends and relatives anxiously waiting at inns and lodges in the valleys below.

No man knew the peaks—the cruel, barren, ice-glazed " roof of Europe "—and what was going on in them, better than Hermann Geiger. And he had unique, superb skill in getting his little plane down amid the tricky, swirling winds and shifting, sloping surfaces of the summits and shoulders.

More than 5,000 times he had landed in the uppermost Alps, and taken off again, without one mishap !

The Piper Cub, which could be fitted with skids, was ideally suited for this strange job. A larger, heavier machine could not have been managed with such delicate precision, would have been more liable to stall and to sink its under-carriage into soft snow. A helicopter could not operate at such heights, and needed a perfectly level surface on which to touch down, but the Cub had a high ceiling and, handled by the gifted Geiger, with his special technique, could be landed on an upward slope, sometimes quite steep, and perhaps uneven. And if it got bogged down in a soft patch, with a little help it could be lifted out.

He regarded himself as a very careful man. He took risks only when a life was in danger—and then they had to be carefully calculated risks, deliberately accepted because of the stakes. He had a wife and a family, he was far from being rich—and the exuberance and opti-mism of youth were behind him. So his mechanics found him fussy about the fine-tuning of the Cub's engine, and no matter how urgent his mission he always made a thorough, calm, pretake-off check of the machine, inside and out.

He practised instrument-flying whenever he could— even on fine, clear days he regularly would pull a canvas sheet over his windscreen and fly " blind " for minutes on end. And in working out his own, extraordinary technique for landing and taking off on tiny, treacherous mountain shelves, this quiet, methodical pilot broke down the problems into scientific terms, studied and mastered the complicated aerodynamics involved.

It never seemed to occur to him that he was running the strangest, and certainly the most successful air rescue service in the world. He was completely, genuinely astonished one day when the authorities informed him that the list of people he had saved from the mountains had reached a total of over three hundred!

Now as he climbed through the deep mattress of cloud, steering the Cub towards the long narrow valley of Zermatt which led to Monte Rosa, he knew how slender were his chances of getting through this time. But at just over 15,000 feet he broke into clear, dazzling sky. Beneath him there were no peaks, no Switzerland—only a vast, unbroken grey sea, stretching into infinity in every direction. Now he began to think how slender were his chances of ever getting *down* again : submerged in that sea of clouds, reaching to within a few hundred feet of the surface, were jagged summits. But this was one of his calculated risks —he was banking on finding a hole in the overcast, somewhere, through which he could descend—grope his way down—before his petrol gave out. Or, if the worst came to the worst, he could always bale out, and perhaps himself finish up lost and hurt, high on some icy tor. . . .

By studying his watch and compass and speed closely, and computing mentally, he tried to keep a rough check on his position as he began to make big, gradually widening circles. After about twenty minutes of this the cloud sagged downward and he saw a great, looming shadow in it— saw it, and with his special knowledge of this wild region instantly recognised it as the Weisshorn. From here, with his position fixed, he was able to fly across to where he knew Monte Rosa must be.

But Monte Rosa had the blankets over her head. He knew she was there, but he couldn't make out even the faintest outline. And if he tried to spiral down through the murk to find her, almost certainly he would see her too late, too close to avoid an annihilating collision. Patience

—that's what was needed now. He settled the Cub into a slow, gentle circle.

Twenty minutes, thirty, forty—and then all at once a rip appeared in the cloud, a rip that widened into a gaping hole. Geiger headed for it, throttled back, dived through the " chimney."

A wandering wind had torn the clouds away from one side of Monte Rosa's crest. He came steeply down and by a stroke of good fortune almost at once saw the hut, and outside it a guide holding at arm's length an ice axe with a handkerchief attached—an improvised windsock, indicating the flow of air over the short, steep slope, above a sheer rock face. Geiger levelled out, flew to and fro for three or four minutes, studying the surface with utmost care. Then he drew away, describing a large semi-circle, losing height.

Heading back towards the short slope, once on a level with it, he tilted the Cub's nose up, adding power. " Hanging on the prop " he let her drop. The ski-undercarriage touched at a point where the slope was almost 30 degrees. *Swoosh*, *who-oomph*—the steepness cut the speed rapidly, the Cub came to rest in less than a hundred yards. Geiger's special technique. . . .

Out of the hut the guide and his comrades carried the muffled, rigid, stretcher-strapped burden. Gently the load was put aboard. Then, directed by Geiger, they lifted the Cub's tail, swung her round to face in the opposite direction.

The take-off was as easy—or as difficult, and dangerous— as falling off a cliff. Geiger opened the throttle, let her slide down the slope and drop over the edge of the vertical rock wall. The Cub dived into space, picked up speed. He eased her out of the dive, and to his immense relief found he was under the belly of the cloud, about a hundred feet above the floor of the valley.

That homeward flight was torture—"like crawling through a tunnel on hands and knees, not knowing when the roof might come down and make it impossible to proceed." The valley was narrow, twisting suddenly, unexpectedly. At times he was only forty feet above the cluttered, crevassed ground. The man in the back lay still, silent, but when Geiger glanced over his shoulder the pale lips tried to pull into a smile. . . .

Sleet again. Memory more than sight moved the controls, steered the little plane round the jutting elbows of rock, raised her over the sudden snags. At times she squeezed through narrow gulches, wing-tips grazing granite walls.

The cloud kept pressing down, trying to squash them into the rugged ground. They flew across a scarred glacier so low that Geiger imagined he could feel the ancient, deathly chill, found himself shivering violently in the cockpit.

Sweat ran down his face, quickly froze into a clamping mask. Concentrating desperately, he recalled the geography of each writhing gorge, banked round giant claws of rock, lifted the Cub over reaching reefs. His wrists and ankles and knees ached, his tendons were taut and strained. He knew he couldn't go on like this much longer, flying an obstacle race, trying to think faster than the next bend or barricade or bluff.

And then suddenly the ground dipped, smoothed out—they were flying down the gradually widening Rhône Valley. The lights of Sion probed through the sleet. As the Cub's skids touched the air-strip's level ground an ambulance came racing across the grass to take Geiger's passenger to hospital. For just a moment the pilot, bruised and exhausted, thought he ought to go too, but the best treatment was administered by a member of his ground crew : " Well done, Hermann ! Well done again. . . ."

He drank a mug of coffee and went home to sleep—before the next phone call.

Captain Jack Slade of the Northern Territory Aerial Medical Services circled low over the flood-bound homestead deep in Australia's Outback. Even during the dry season there was no landing strip here. Now, after the big rains, there was only the immense, silent, slow-swirling, brown blanket of water—and the mud. Thick, soft, treacherous . . .

Somehow Slade had to find a landing ground. Down in that lonely homestead a child lay sick. Minutes counted.

Five slow, searching circuits—and then he saw the narrow oblong of grass humping out of the flood waters. An overgrown peanut patch, with trees all around it . . . not much, but the only possible landing place in hundreds of miles. He knew he must risk it.

He went down, put her into a wide, slow turn, and made a close inspection of the surface: rough, but it looked solid enough. He pulled up again, and started a careful, slow approach.

On board with him was Nursing Sister "Billy " Hill. This was her first trip, and she had been miserably sick in the bumpy flying conditions. Now she'd drowsed off to sleep, wan and exhausted. He didn't wake her—not even when he'd touched down and, rolling and lurching along, realised that he had only about four hundred yards left in which to pull up. Plainly, there was no hope. And if he tried to swing round, the plane might overturn, or

" ground loop "—in which case the nurse could be injured and unable to tend her young patient.

Only one thing to do—he'd let her run straight into the trees at the end of the paddock, and hope nothing too drastic happened. So he sat there, watching the barrier rush towards him, trying not to go rigid and " freeze " on the controls. He aimed the plane between two giant trees. Only when the massive trunks—just far enough apart for the fuselage to get through—sliced off the wings, did Sister Hill wake up.

She peered out of the cabin windows and said placidly : " Wot . . . no wings ?"

They waded through the floods to the homestead, and Sister Hill began the fight to save the baby. But it was too late : the child died half-an-hour later.

Not all stories of endeavour and self-sacrifice end in success. When you battle daily against the realities of huge distances, harsh climate and some of the wildest country on earth, you have to expect setbacks, failures—and some disasters.

The pilots and medical staff of Australia's Royal Flying Doctor Service—to which the Northern Territory Aerial Medical Services is a companion organisation—look upon floods, dust storms, the lack of landing strips, the hazards of navigating across whole states to pin-point some tiny building on a featureless landscape, as all in the day's toil. Routine. Such men as Captain Slade, and women like Sister Hill, are carrying on the work of compassion started back in 1928 by the Very Reverend John Flynn. A Presbyterian missionary, Flynn became a legend in his own lifetime for his work in the loneliest inland regions of central and Northern Australia.

About 1911, the young Flynn went out to join the

pioneers who were struggling to force a living from the reluctant Outback. He came to know these courageous and resourceful people well—and he realised the terrible fear that constantly nagged at them. The fear of being struck down by sickness or accident, in areas where the nearest doctor was weeks away. In those days Death always travelled faster than help.

But after World War One, two scientific developments began to re-shape the living patterns of the world—aviation and radio. The young Outback clergyman immediately saw the possibilities for Australia. " Flynn of the Inland " set out to spread, in his own phrase, " a mantle of safety " over the inhospitable deserts. His zeal and vision fired other men. By 1928 his dream had come true, when the first Flying Doctor base was set up at Cloncurry, in North-West Queensland.

By the time Flynn died in 1951, Australia had six bases. Today there are fourteen, covering some 2,000,000 square miles, or two-thirds of the continent.

In 1960, from the twelve mainland bases—there are two in Tasmania—1,612 flights covering 594,653 miles were made ; 1,292 patients were transported, and 11,754 medical consultations were given by radio. In addition, the doctors flew thousands of miles on routine visits, and bringing preventive medicine to people in the Outback.

The radio networks have long operated beyond their original, basic purpose—they have become the schools through which lonely children are taught, and the back-yard fences over which news and family gossip are ex-changed to lighten the isolation of the empty spaces.

The doctors and nurses, too, do other jobs outside of medicine. In remote areas, they are sometimes called upon to act as judges, government officials, arbiters—any representative of authority who might be needed. On record is a report from a Flying Doctor which reads:

Flew to Marble Bar, saw twelve patients, performed two operations, held an inquest, conducted a court case, pulled teeth, renewed hotel licence, granted applications for mining leases and permits to employ local labour.

Flew home for tea.

The former Governor General of Australia, the late Viscount Dunrossil, described this unique organisation as: " This wonderful service—a combination of medical, aeronautical and radio skill and enterprise that has leapt over distances to bring a really Australian answer, idealistic but intensely practical, to an Australian problem."

The whole history of flying, in peace and in war, is enriched by dramatic, valiant rescue operations—flights of mercy through furious weather, to bring medical aid or food to isolated communities ; helicopters descending through skies full of searching metal to evacuate wounded in the midst of battle ; seaplanes and flying boats risking disintegration to touch down on high-heaving seas and pick up shipwrecked sailors ; long, desperate searches in blizzard, rainstorm or mist, by day and by night, for missing ships, planes, climbers, explorers, prospectors. . . .

A bulky, busy book could be written on this theme alone—the stories of those twentieth century life-savers who, in keeping with one of mankind's most ancient symbols, have descended, godlike, to bring succour from the heavens. But here I have been able to mention only a few of the many who fly, not to fight, but to save ; not in combat, but in compassion.

CHAPTER SEVENTEEN

SKYMEN FROM DOWN-UNDER

THE VAST, sun-baked crowds out at Brisbane's Eagle Farm Airport were having a day of air thrills—spectacle, speed, stunning sound. They clapped their hands over their ears as the huge, majestic turbo-jet airliner screamed past just above them, then marvelled at the nerveless precision flying of the Meteor fighters as they dived, rolled, flashed over the field in the five-star formation of the Southern Cross—symbolic constellation of the Antipodes.

As the formation passed, and the deep rumble of the jet engines faded, a silence fell. Then someone looked up, and a single, silver-glinting speck moving slowly across the dazzling sky caught his attention. He pointed, laughed, and soon everyone was watching the tiny, old " steam " plane 9,000 feet above them. Suddenly thick white smoke plumed out behind it, and the sea of upturned faces followed it as, in a series of leisurely loops and swooping dives it traced out a single word, vivid white against the blue. A word which raised from the throats of those watching thousands a roar almost as mighty as the jets' thunder of moments before—

" SMITHY "

The sky-writing was apt tribute, on that day in August 1958, to an Australian who some thirty years before had endured untold hours of pain and peril to pioneer air routes all over the world—Sir Charles Kingsford Smith.

And now the machine in which he had battled and groped through so many miles of uncharted, often hostile sky—the three-engined, high-winged Fokker monoplane "Southern Cross"—was being officially installed in a permanent home. She would be preserved for all time in an imposing structure of glass and timber only yards from the spot where she had touched down—on what was then little more than a dusty paddock—after Smithy's epic first crossing of the Pacific Ocean in 1928.

Born in Brisbane, Queensland, in 1897, Kingsford Smith showed an early taste for imaginative and dangerous escapades. When he was just six the family sailed for a visit to Canada, and in mid-ocean he was found hanging from a hawse-hole at the ship's bows, showing another boy how it could be done.

At eighteen he enlisted in the Australian infantry. He served as a dispatch-rider in Egypt, Gallipoli and France. And then he transferred to the Royal Flying Corps, in which he was commissioned in 1917.

The trainee pilot showed an immediate aptitude and was quick to learn. Though there was one little setback. A cryptic entry in his logbook at the end of his basic training read : " First solo—crashed ! "

Coming in after his first lone circuit of the field he had made a perfect three-point touchdown—fifteen feet up in the air. The aircraft was a complete write-off, but even the severe knocks and bruises, and the blow to his career, didn't stop Smithy laughing. Throughout his life, he was ever able to enjoy a joke against himself—and it was said that he never waited for others to tell the tales of his misadventures.

He arrived back in Australia after the war—minus three toes, but plus the Military Cross. He was smouldering with ideas and eagerness. Flying was in his blood now, and he had been quick to realise that Australia, with its horizonless tracts of emptiness separating fast-growing towns and cities, *needed* aviation. Air communications could bring the vast continent to the full realisation of its potential, knitting its widely-dispersed centres into a virile, purposeful pattern. And no more would Australians feel remote, cut off from the rest of the civilised world—for aircraft could span the seas as well as the " Outback."

With C. P. T. Ulm as partner, Kingsford Smith set about the task—planning the routes, persuading people to start air companies. Success was slow and sporadic: money was hard to raise in those post-war days. Generous by nature, but with no business head, he fretted at the delays. Air lines would be formed, they would stumble along a while—and go broke. Another round of fund-raising, of working at any job that came along—anything to raise cash. Then the setting up of a new company: and the whole cycle would be restarted. But the nation wasn't air-minded yet, so customers were few.

" What we need," Smithy said to Ulm one despondent day, " is something to make 'em really sit up and take notice. Just one record-breaking flight, that's all it needs—then the funds and the bookings would start pouring in."

Ulm saw the sense. Every shilling they had left went into the gamble. They went to America to raise the rest, and on 31st May, 1928, the " Southern Cross " took off from Oakland, California, for the first-ever flight over 8,000 miles of Pacific Ocean to Australia. And even as she lumbered fully-laden down the runway, creditors were urgently elbowing through the crowds to have Smithy arrested for debt. . . .

The little Fokker plane—17 feet 8½ inches wingspan,

its three Whirlwind engines each developing 200 horse power—was by no means new. She had already given noble service to Sir Hubert Wilkins during his Arctic explorations, but with her crew of four—Ulm was second pilot; Americans Harry Lyon and James Warner had joined the venture as navigator and wireless operator—she was facing her toughest test, and many believed it would prove too much for " a worn machine."

Hour after hour, day after day, Smithy and his crew droned on, hopping great distances from island to tiny hard-to-find island; cramped, noise-numbed, buffeted by winds and rains. Eventually, the longest hop of all: over 3,000 miles of trackless sea to Suva. Thirty-three hours it took them, and most of the time they were weaving around, making rapid, often huge diversions to avoid vicious squalls. Harry Lyon's superb navigation stood the test: out of all the ocean, after all those confusing course changes—there was Suva, dead ahead.

Their tired hearts sang—until they sighted Albert Park, the only possible landing space. It was incredibly small, bumpy—and entirely surrounded by tall trees and telegraph lines . . .

Smithy groaned, and braced his stiff, weary body.

Throttle back—steady—ease her in just over—cut ! stall !—drop her in !

No one could have judged it more accurately : even so, there seemed no chance of stopping her rolling in time to avoid the trees at the other end. Smithy made his decision : *quick swerve !—full throttle on the starboard motor—full left rudder !*

She wheeled to the left, the port wingtip grazed the ground, and she finished up spinning in a terrific " ground loop ". When the whorl of dust settled the damage proved

slight—nothing compared to what would have been caused
by running into the trees. It is still talked of as one of the
epic landings of all time. Certainly it was only Kingsford
Smith's skill and coolness that saved " Southern Cross "
that day, and enabled them—when some of the taller
trees had been felled—to get out again and finally arrive,
battered and weary, at Brisbane on 9th June.

The flight resulted in £20,000 being subscribed for
Kingsford Smith and Ulm to finance other pioneering
flights across the world, many of them in the same " worn
machine ".

The record books can tell only the barest facts. The
same year, a first Australia-New Zealand flight ; 1929,
Sydney (Australia) to Croydon ; 1930, light aircraft
England-Australia solo record ; 1931, first official Australia-
England air mail flight ; 1931 again, and another Australia-
England trip, this time alone ; two years later, the return
trip, in the record time of seven days, four hours, 44
minutes ; 1934, the first West-East Pacific flight, this time
in a single-engined Lockheed Altair.

The bare facts. With no hint of the conditions under
which the flights were made. Whatever aircraft he flew—
and mostly it was the faithful old " Southern Cross "
—and whether he was alone, or with Ulm or others, every
one of those entries in the Kingsford Smith log book was
written only after many days and nights of intense concentration, and physical and nervous strain—sitting cramped,
ears and senses beaten, blurred by the never-ending roar
of engines. After agonised hours, with eyes burning from
constant searching for landmarks after sleepless nights :
hours of harrowing anxiety over the uncertainties of
navigating across featureless sea and uncharted land,
every moment watching water and clouds for the slightest

wind changes, constantly calculating petrol and oil consumption, wondering whether he had enough left to get
him to that day's refuelling stop : dragging, draining hours
of sheer bone-weariness and—on the solo flights—desperate loneliness. His string of triumphs justly earned him
a knighthood. But that didn't change the warm, simple
character of the man. And he didn't rest on his fame and
honours.

Once, over Turkey, he felt himself fainting at the
controls. That night when he landed the police jailed
him, and kept him there for four days—something was wrong
with his papers. They probably saved his life, for the doctors later found he had been suffering from carbon mon-
oxide poisoning from leaking petrol fumes. On returning
to his plane he spotted the broken pipe and had it repaired.

Kingsford Smith was a man of tremendous, consuming
determination, great stamina and courage. And he was
always completely honest about his own weaknesses,
errors and doubts. Take a look through his own log of
the England-Australia solo flight in 1933. He had taken
off on 4th October in a Percival Gull, and was soon writing
of himself as " a case of nerves ", " terribly sick ". He
had to be careful not to fly too high, in case he passed out
at the controls. There is a frank, human ring to many of
these entries, scribbled on his knee as he flew :

2nd day. 6.40 a.m. Passing Athens. Still getting these
nervous attacks. Guess I'm too old and worn for these capers.

At 36, he felt " too old and worn . . ." An indication of
how much these trail-blazing flights took out of the man.

Later : Another recurrence of nervousness . . . nasty feeling I
was going to faint. Hope I can get through !

October 7. Landed Gwadar (on the Arabian Sea). Terribly
sick at 4.15 p.m. yesterday. Couldn't sleep till 2 a.m. No

*food now for 36 hours. Left Gwadar 7.15. Beautiful morning
but failed to appreciate it. Wish I was reliable as this machine
and engine . . . 4 p.m. Rested at Karachi four hours but can't
sleep. This is what is killing me. Got some bromide here and
will take a stiff dose tonight.*

*October 8. Another night with not much sleep. How long
can I stick it?*

Later that day, he realised he was over the halfway mark,
and from there on the entries cheer up. But he had flown
the 6,000 miles from Brindisi in Italy with nine hours sleep
in three nights, and almost no food. Small wonder that
the last entry reads :

*Am all in, but today is the last day. Have just to hang on
somehow for 9 hours.*

Hang on he did, and the record was his.

The story was always the same, flight after flight. But
the hard flying, and the ever-present financial difficulties
took their toll. In 1935 he planned a new attempt on the
England-Australia record, this time in an Altair aircraft.
His old flying partner Ulm had been lost some 500 miles
north of Hawaii on a trans-Pacific flight the year before,
and he took with him J. T. Pethybridge. Shortly before the
trip Kingsford Smith, with his usual frankness, confessed :
" I don't feel fit enough for the job, but I'm going to see
it through."

He wasn't being melodramatic or foolhardy ; it was
just his old, ceaseless urge to overcome the weakness of
the flesh. Did that worn-out, battered spirit fail, just for
once ? Did his over-taxed body finally collapse ? Or was
it a technical fault in the plane ? We shall never know.
They found the wreckage off the Burma coast . . . but no
trace was ever found of the two occupants. All we do know
is that, some time on the 7th or 8th of November, 1935,

Sir Charles Kingsford Smith, airman supreme and pioneer extraordinary, died at his controls.

15th May, 1943—the atmosphere on the bomber base at Scampton, in the heart of England's flat, bleak Midlands, was tense—and getting tenser. For weeks the squadron, newly-formed from the crack crews of the R.A.F.'s Bomber Command, had been training in their big four-engined Lancasters. Hour after hour, by day and by night, they had been practising low-level flying, roaring over England at less than 100 feet. And they had been drilled in a new bombing technique which entailed flying at 60 feet—precisely—above water, and aiming through a strange, Heath Robinson device of wood and nails instead of an orthodox bomb-sight.

The Lancs had been specially modified. The crews were so highly trained by now that it was said they could navigate at hedgetop level to any given tree in the country, and hit any minor crossroads with their practice bombs. Still the only man in the squadron to know the purpose of all this was the commander. Everyone else knew only that something out of the ordinary was about to happen—soon. The arrival of the new, huge bombs, strangely shaped, only heightened the tension, increased the rumours.

And then one morning: " Attention . . . All pilots, navigators and bomb-aimers of 617 report to the briefing room immediately." The blaring tannoy brought a sudden knot to the stomach, a dryness to the throat. Each of the flyers answering the summons was secretly wondering whether he would be alive after the next forty-eight hours . . .

By lunch-time, they were back in the mess ; they knew now, but were forbidden to tell the other members of their crews. The show was " on "—for to-morrow night.

The others—the gunners, the engineers, the wireless operators—had been waiting anxiously. One of them, Australian Toby Foxlee, eagerly sought out his skipper, Micky Martin.

" Well, what's it all about ? "

" Just more training, Foxy," Martin said as casually as he could. " You'll hear all about it to-morrow."

" Training ? I don't believe it ! "

" It's true, boy."

" Aw, come off it, Skip ! Give us the straight gen."

" I swear it."

Foxlee stared hard, then mouthed an oath. " In that case, I need a drink. You ? "

" Shandy," said Martin. Foxlee swung back, eyes small and bright. He knew Martin liked his beer by the pint—but never did any hard drinking before an op.

" Skipper," said the gunner, " you're a horrible ruddy liar."

And the very next night Wing Commander Guy Gibson, D.S.O., D.F.C., led 617 to the Moehne, Eder and Sorpe dams, deep in Germany. One of the greatest air operations in history : the exploit which earned the squadron its glorious nickname, " The Dam Busters ".

Flying alongside Gibson was Micky Martin, in his faithful Lancaster P-Peter (which he irreverently insisted on calling P-Popsie). Born in Sydney twenty-four years before, Martin—tall, fair and slim, with a generous moustache—had done all his war-time flying with the R.A.F. And he had become addicted to, and expert in, the art of low flying. His thinking was supremely simple : if you flew lower than the rest of the bombers in the stream, usually you avoided the enemy fighters ; lower still, and the heavy anti-aircraft fire would burst well above you; right down to tree-top level, and you would be gone before the light stuff could draw a bead on you—and your gunners had a high old time picking off searchlights and any other targets offered. There was, of course, the risk of being cleaved by the cable of a barrage balloon, but Martin figured that no one put up balloons along main roads and railways—so he flew up those. . . .

All very fine in theory, but a very different matter when it comes to handling a fully-laden, four-engined bomber through hostile night across enemy territory. That calls for rock nerves, instantaneous reflexes—all the highest skills. And Martin had them in plenty. Which is why Gibson had picked him for 617. They'd met at Buckingham Palace, when Gibson was getting his D.S.O. and Martin the first of his D.F.C.s, and they'd talked about low flying. At once Gibson recognised a bomber captain of outstanding talent. The exactly right combination of daring and caution.

True, on the ground Martin had a wild look in his eyes, and he indulged in horseplay and all sorts of escapades. But in the air he was calm and crisp, took no *needless* risks. Early in his operational career he had made up his mind that he was going to die before the war ended, and die unpleasantly, probably trapped in a blazing Lancaster. Having accepted that, he began to live life to the absolute fullest, and in his off-duty hours quickly gained a reputation for boisterousness. But the moment he climbed into his aircraft, he settled down to earnest, professional work. He did his job to the utmost, completely reconciled to the idea that it would kill him. The object of the grim game was to see how long you could delay the pay-off.

When necessary, Martin was audacious—but in a calcula-

ting way. Every risk was measured : he meant to spin
out his life as long as he could, and every single bomb tell
while he lasted.

Micky Martin survived the great dams raid, and was
awarded the D.S.O. Other Australians also came through—
the incredibly boyish Dave Shannon (he celebrated his
21st birthday a few days later, and went on to win a bar
to his D.S.O., plus a couple of D.F.C.s), and Les Knight.
In Martin's own crew there were long-chinned Jack
Leggo, the navigator, and Bob Hay, the bomb-aimer,
who won bars to their D.F.C.s. Among the total of ten
D.F.C.s was Gibson's own bomb-aimer, the chunky
Australian " Spam " Spafford. Two C.G.M.s and twelve
D.F.M.s completed the decorations won that famous night
plus Gibson's own Victoria Cross.

Martin, in fact, to his own surprise, survived every raid
he went out on. But death grazed by many times—
notably in 617's third attempt on the difficult and heavily
defended Antheor Viaduct in Italy, when P-Popsie was
badly shot up while he was doing impossible things with
her in the face of murderous flak. Coming down to almost
zero feet to mark the target with flares for the other planes,
it seemed that no aircraft could live through the tight
cross-fire from batteries all around the target—some of
them actually *firing down* on to the marauder. But the tiny
koala bear mascot Martin always stuffed into his battledress
just before take-off saw them safely through the inferno.
And they left the target brightly outlined by their flares.

Limping away, they listed the damage : first they
found the port inner and starboard outer throttles gone,
and the pitch controls for the other two engines gone too—
so they had just enough power to keep the bomber airborne. A shell had smashed through the nose and exploded

in the ammo. trays under the front turret : in the ensuing blasts and flarings of bullets, hydraulic pipes, control rods and fuse boxes were all hit. Two of the crew were wounded, and so was Martin himself—in the leg. Obviously they were out of the fight—if they took her in again to drop their bombs with the others, she would be slow and unweildy and might impede and endanger their comrades. And certainly they would be hit again : no aircraft could survive any more hurt and stay airborne. So Martin pulled her up and began to battle for altitude.

Not a hope of getting home—that was grimly clear right away. They set course for Corsica, only just occupied by the Allies. But the plane became increasingly sluggish. Someone came back from a further investigation, with news that the entire hydraulic systems were useless.

"You'll probably get your undercarriage and flaps down, by the manual emergency system, but you won't have any brakes to pull up with once we're on the deck," he told Martin.

Then another of the crew brought an even more chilling report : "The fuses have had it, and we've still got the bombs on board." A faulty landing, and they'd end in an annihilating explosion . . .

They were at 2,000 feet now, with little prospect of getting higher. They had on board, fused and live, a 4,000 pound bomb and several 1,000 pounders—and the minimum safety height for dropping a 4,000 pounder was 4,000 feet. Any lower, and you got caught in the blast yourself.

Rain came, and then hail. Water was flooding in through the tail—and then they ran into an ice cloud. The wounded Martin felt the controls grow even more soggy. Every moment now he was fighting to keep his height. The crew managed to cut one of the smaller bombs loose, but as it fell Popsie stalled. The starboard wingtip dropped, and they were on the verge of a spin. Somehow Martin regained control—but now they were down to 1,800 feet . . .

Still, they were 1,000 pounds lighter. Slowly, brilliantly, he coaxed her up again. At 2,500 feet two more of the 1,000 pounders were dropped. But they needed still more height before they could get rid of the big one.

A long, sweating, agonising haul took her to 3,200 feet. And then it was plain that she had reached her limit— she was still in the climbing attitude, but not moving any higher. After a conference it was decided that it would be safer to risk dropping the 4,000 pounder from this height, than to try to land with it still "hung up" in the bomb bay. As it left the aircraft, Popsie jumped weakly. She jumped again like a frightened mule when the shock wave of the explosion reached her, but Martin caught her smartly with rudder and they were straight and level again.

But nothing would shift the two remaining 1,000 pounders.

A little later the airstrip on Corsica radioed that there were better medical facilities at a field in Sardinia, and a new course was set. Martin grinned sardonically when he heard that the best approach was over a range of mountains 8,000 feet high, and set about planning his own, lower route in.

They found the field. It ran *across* a narrow spit of land—the runway started at the beach and stopped abruptly at a cliff edge.

When you still have two fused 1,000 pound bombs on board, a belly-landing is ruled out. Then again, the undercarriage might go down, or it might not; the tyres might be all right, or they might be ripped by shrapnel —in which case the plane stood a good chance of ground-looping, so that they could easily collapse on to the bombs. And there was no question of going round again. Everything had to be right first time, for there wasn't enough power left in the damaged engines to climb again for a second approach.

Their chances—after the hours of struggle—seemed very small. But no one wanted to bale-out and leave the wounded men. They'd all see it through together.

Martin started his preparations early. Slowly the undercart swung down, and seemed to stick in place. There was just enough pressure to get some flap down. Martin—muscles aching, throbbing from the tussle of keeping the shattered Lancaster in the air, and his wounded leg feeling oddly numb—headed in on a long, low approach from miles back. At the last moment he cut all engines and pulled the nose up to clear the dunes. At about 85 m.p.h. she squashed down on to the runway. The undercart held, Martin began fish-tailing his rudders. The far cliff loomed alarmingly, and he pushed on full port rudder.

The broken bomber swung sickeningly, jolted over the grass verge. She started to slew, tyres skidding just short of a ground-loop—and came to a lumbering halt fifty yards from the precipice . . .

Bob Hay was dead. Whittaker, the engineer, had come within an ace of losing a leg. Martin, who during the whole of this superb feat of flying had been imagining himself seriously wounded, found that in fact his leg had barely been punctured. His main injury was a huge, numbing bruise.

When they got back to England days later, it was to

find they had been posted off operations. Martin argued furiously, but he found himself behind a desk at Group H.Q. Not for long, though—very quickly he had fixed himself another posting, this time to a Mosquito night-fighter unit. And this man who fully expected to die in the air —who at times seemed to be seeking every opportunity to fly into the highest peril—in fact survived the war, finishing up with a D.S.O. and bar, D.F.C. and two bars.

Group Captain Leonard Cheshire, V.C., D.S.O. and two bars, D.F.C., who led 617 after Gibson, once wrote this of Micky Martin : " As an operational pilot I consider he was . . . the greatest that the Air Force ever produced. I have seen him do things that I, for one, would never have looked at." Coming from as great and brave a pilot as Cheshire, that is a remarkable tribute to a remarkable man.

Martin was one of many Australians who served in the R.A.F. Thousands more came to Britain in the R.A.A.F., and the distinctive, dark blue, " digger " uniforms were familiar all over the country. They had first been seen in " the old country " back in July 1939, when seven officers and fourteen airmen arrived to ferry back nine Sunderland flying boats to help in the defence of the Commonwealth against the looming threat of war. But before they had learned to fly them, war was declared—and they stayed to form the nucleus of No. 10 Squadron, R.A.A.F.

They were quickly joined by an ever-growing stream of their countrymen. They operated in every Command. The R.A.A.F.'s first D.F.C. was awarded in July 1940 to Squadron Leader C. W. Pearce, of 10 Squadron, after he had attacked a submarine in the Atlantic.

They won two V.C.s in the air over Europe. The first was awarded to Group Captain Hughie Idwal Edwards, a Western Australian who had joined the R.A.F. before the war. On 4th July, 1941, he led a force of Blenheim bombers on a daylight attack on the port of Bremen, one of the most heavily defended areas of Germany.

The squadron flew the last fifty miles to the target at little more than fifty feet, passing under high-tension cables, and finally weaving through a thick balloon barrage. On through what seemed a solid wall of flak—*every aircraft was hit.* But they pressed home the assault, led all the way by the dark, thickset Australian.

The citation which resulted said that Edwards had displayed " the highest possible standards of gallantry and determination."

A little over a year later, on 28th November, 1942, 26-year-old Pilot Officer Rawdon Hume Middleton, R.A.A.F., of New South Wales, was piloting a Stirling bomber over Turin in Italy. The flight over the 12,000 foot barrier of the Alps had been difficult and exhausting, and above the target the plane was hit by A.A. fire. A large piece was blasted out of the port wing, and another shell burst inside the cockpit, shattering the windscreen. A splinter took away part of Middleton's face, destroying his right eye. It is probable that he had other wounds, in the chest—there was no way of checking. He lost consciousness and the plane dived to 800 feet before the second pilot—wounded in head and legs—regained control. Somehow Middleton fought through the nausea and waves of pain to take over again. And despite the savage, ice-barbed wind screaming in through the shattered wind-screen, he insisted on tackling once again the Alpine crossing.

His one aim was to reach England so that his crew could bale-out ; he must have known that because of his wounds, the severe loss of blood and his fast-diminishing strength, there was little chance of saving himself. He settled down to coax the last ounce of power out of the damaged bomber, the last degree of concentration out of his failing body and clouding mind . . .

Four hours later, they were over the French coast. And again they were hit by flak. Somehow Middleton summoned the strength to take evasive action, and they wriggled out of the claws of the guns, reaching the English coast with exactly five minutes' fuel left.

Middleton flew parallel to the coast for a few miles, looking down with dimming eyes at the quiet shores, and the fields misted in the early daylight. Then quietly, firmly, he said goodbye to his crew, ordered them to jump. He circled, watched them land safely on the shore. Then he headed out to sea, to die alone with his crippled bomber.

In every phase of the flying war, both in Europe and the Pacific, Australian airmen played a vital part, flyers and ground crews alike. The individual tales of gallantry are endless—more than 3,000 R.A.A.F. men were decorated overseas, another 1,000 in the Australian theatre. Every story has the ring of that same high spirit and self-reliance which has been part of the Aussie character since the days of the hardy pioneers and explorers of the Outback.

And that spirit is perhaps best illustrated by a photograph on the files of the Air Ministry. Taken in London just after the shooting had stopped in Europe in 1945, it shows two young R.A.A.F. pilots, leaning against the bonnet of a sports car, grinning at each other. Both had flown on many ops., and each had been taken prisoner.

Turn the picture over, and the caption gives you their names: Flying Officer Peter Kingsford Smith, D.F.C. (one of three of the great Smithy's nephews who served with distinction in the R.A.A.F. during the war), and

Pilot Officer John Anthony Ulm, son of Smithy's navigator and co-pilot back in the trail-blazing days.

New Zealand doesn't claim much of the world map: just two slim, curving islands deep in the Pacific, with a population even now of only 2,400,000. But its people are no back-yard dreamers; isolated they may be in some ways—but insular, no.

Witness the deed of Richard Pearse, of Temuka in South Island, a taciturn farmer who liked working by himself. In a quaint contraption of his own design, he flew a hundred yards, landing on top of a twelve-foot hedge. The date: March 1904—*only three months after the Wright Brothers had made the first powered flight of history.* . . .

If the belief that Pearse took off under his own power is correct, then he was indeed an epic pioneer—for the Wright plane had to be launched by catapult. Certainly the Temuka farmer was the first man in all the British Commonwealth to fly in a heavier-than-air machine.

Witness, too, the devouring eagerness with which the slim and attractive young daughter of a Rotorua dental surgeon followed the newspaper stories of Bert Hinkler's flight in 1928. She had never flown, but Hinkler's adventures, unfolding day by day, fired her ambition. Within a few years, those same newspapers were carrying reports and pictures of the dentist's daughter, and the slender figure in immaculate white overalls and flying helmet became familiar the world over.

Jean Batten was just twenty when she travelled to England, chaperoned by her mother, her mind and heart set on flying back to Australia. Coolly she told reporters that she'd learned to fly " expressly for this trip." The experts tried to talk her out of the project—dangerous even for a fully experienced male pilot. She smiled, politely, thanked them for their concern—and proceeded with her plans.

She took off from Lympne, Kent, on 9th April, 1933. All went well as far as Karachi, when her engine failed. She crash-landed, and her frail aircraft was a complete write-off. Many thought the experience would "knock some sense" into this imprudent, inexperienced lass. But Jean smiled, said she'd start all over again. Back to England, another hard, often discouraging round of money-raising, and then just over a year later she was off again in a battered old Gypsy Moth.

Disaster again. This time at Rome. But Jean borrowed new wings and flew the plane back to start the whole process for the third time. . . .

Years later, talking of this sad train of events, she admitted : " A great deal of my *enthusiasm* for the flight had gone—but I'd doubled my determination."

In May, 1934, she took off once more. At last, complete success—she landed at Darwin 14 days, 22 hours and thirty minutes later, and had the welcoming crowds wondering how she could appear so femininely neat and trim after such an exhausting solitary journey. They weren't the last crowd to ask this question.

With the women's solo U.K.-Australia record in her pocket (four-and-a-half days under Amy Johnson's time), within a year she became the first woman to make the return flight ; and soon after that she set up a record time of two days, thirteen hours and fifteen minutes for the U.K.-Brazil flight, and became the first woman to fly solo across the South Atlantic.

But perhaps the flight that most enslaved public imagination was her crossing of the Tasman Sea in 1936. Over

1,000 miles of open, shark-infested waters. With radio in its infancy, and aircraft still small, slow and far from reliable, it was a formidable undertaking—one that had daunted many men. Jean Batten was resolved not only to be the first woman to fly it alone—she meant also to do it in record time.

She had already set up a world record for the UK-Australia trip, with five days, twenty-one-and-a-half hours—beating Jim Broadbent's time by close on one day. Now she flew down to Sydney to complete the flight home—the first direct U.K.-New Zealand flight ever.

After two days of fêting, she flew down to Richmond, 40 miles west of Sydney, to make her final preparations. The Richmond field had a longer runway and was thus safer for taking-off in a plane heavy with extra fuel. Once again people, including seasoned pilots, tried to talk her out of the venture, but when favourable weather came, she took off at 4.35 in the morning, refusing the offer of a radio set because of the extra weight, but gratefully accepting a packet of ham and lettuce sandwiches, a flask of coffee and two oranges.

Half Australia and all New Zealand held their breath when the news that she was airborne came through—the thoughts of thousands were with her in that tiny throbbing cockpit, an utterly lonely little world of its own, bobbing, lurching on so slowly above that barren, killer sea. A ten-hour flight was her aim : it was just nine-and-a-half hours and one ferocious rainstorm later that she crossed her homeland coast at New Plymouth.

While the news that she had been sighted flashed around the globe, she flew on to Auckland. There she received her greatest welcome—and a fatherly admonition from the Mayor, " for giving the country such an anxious time."

By now Jean Batten—still only 27—was being honoured by cities, and mobbed by the public. Everywhere people marvelled at the immense spirit and professionalism that drove this gently-natured, fragile-looking girl. They loved her too, for her constant femininity—whenever she stepped from her plane, no matter how long and arduous the flight, she always managed to look *chic* in her white overalls. It was common knowledge that as she came into an airfield, just before she began her landing approach she would add a freshening touch of powder and lipstick.

The dentist's daughter caught the headlines year after year until finally she gave up flying. But she was by no means the only New Zealander to claim a proud place for her country in the history of aviation.

When World War Two came, flying had caught the interest and imagination of thousands of young men in the islands. Yet in September 1939, the R.N.Z.A.F. comprised only 37 officers and 302 other ranks. But in the first weeks of hostilities, thousands flooded in to volunteer, so that by July 1944 the total strength was 42,000.

Soon twenty-six New Zealand squadrons were on service, scattered throughout the world. In addition many thousands of New Zealanders were serving with R.A.F. units, on both ground and flying duties.

Men like Flying Officer E. J. (" Cobber ") Kain, the black-haired, blue-eyed, six foot tall fighter star from Wellington—mentioned in an earlier chapter of this book.

And like Sergeant Pilot J. A. Ward, a 22-year-old from Wanganui, who won New Zealand's first Victoria Cross of World War Two. His Wellington bomber of No. 73 (N.Z.) Squadron was badly hit by a night-fighter while returning from a raid on Munster. Fire broke out close to the starboard engine, and was fed by petrol from a split pipe. Something decisive, perhaps drastic, was called for if they were not all to end up in the Zuider Zee thousands of feet below—and Ward knew seconds counted.

Coolly he volunteered to climb out along the wing, to put out the flames.

His skipper had to *order* him to take his parachute out with him as he clambered through the narrow astro-hatch into the howling night, and clawed his way down the three foot drop on to the wing. Clinging on with one hand he hacked footholds in the plane's fabric with the other, inched his way along the screaming, wind-lashed wing, out to the fire.

The gale gripped him like a giant fist of ice. The cold tore through his clothing, numbing the muscles, probing for his bones. It was a battle to breathe. And then, suddenly, the hot, thick fumes from the fire were stabbing into his mouth and eyes, blinding, choking. . . .

But he beat out the flames somehow, then stopped up the leaking pipe with a piece of rag. No more roasting blast—he was freezing again, in an ice-barbed hurricane. How he managed to drag himself back, he could never remember. But he made it to safety, and so did the bomber.

After the award was announced, Ward was alarmed and embarrassed by the publicity, the " hero " image, the cheering crowds which confronted him on the " personal appearances " at war factories and recruiting centres that inevitably were arranged for him. He hated all " fuss and bull ", and tried every time to dodge it.

But Ward didn't have to put up with fame for long. Two months after his V.C. action, he was shot down and killed over Hamburg.

To survive for long in the air war, a man needed a

charmed life—whatever his skill. One who had plenty of both was a tough New Zealander who had come to Britain and joined the R.A.F. in 1937, and who finished the war as a Wing Commander with the D.S.O., O.B.E., D.F.C. and bar, D.F.C.(U.S.) and the French Croix de Guerre with Plume.

Fighter leader Alan Deere was in the thick of it for most of the war. His face, under the short fair hair, and with the fine straight nose, was as well-known to the free world newspaper readers during the Battle of Britain as were the features of film stars like David Niven and Robert Donat.

Five times he escaped death by incredible fortune. Once German bombers arrived over his airfield just as his squadron was taking off. A bomb landed immediately in front of his plane, sent it Catherine-wheeling, to end up a crumpled mass, upside down, with Deere's head scraping the ground.

He survived several other crashes, and was shot down three times. He had, they said, " the coolest head, and the hottest reflexes, in Fighter Command." And like his friend the great Stanford Tuck, he had an immense amount of luck.

Between September 1939 and May 1944, Deere was credited with more than twenty victories. He then became commander of an advanced airfield of the Allied Expeditionary Air Force during the invasion of Europe. And among the new, young flyers he led to final victory were many from his own country : those small slim, islands of New Zealand, still sparsely populated, but—in this age of flying—no longer remote from the other free nations of the Earth.

CHAPTER EIGHTEEN

CRESCENT WINGS AND AFTER

WAR ALWAYS adds an urgency to scientific research and development. Under stress nothing is spared—vast sums are poured in, the finest brains concentrated. Medicine and surgery are two examples. Aviation is another.

Perhaps ironically, but for the impetus of 1914-18, we probably would still be in the process of emerging from the canvas-and-string days. The sheer, vital necessity in wartime of producing ever-swifter aircraft, easier to handle and more deadly than the enemy's swept the world's aviation industries along on a great floodtide of spectacular, bold, often imprudent advances. And afterwards—when the guns stopped—the leading nations clearly saw the limitless potentialities of peacetime flying.

All through the 'twenties and 'thirties development continued, but at a vastly slower, more cautious pace. Came 1939, and another spurt. By the time the world was at peace again, aviation had made more progress in a shorter time than any other industry before or since.

Think of it. In 1914 men were still taking the first doubtful, hesitant steps off the ground; by 1945, they were confidently controlling huge, complex machines at speeds and heights which their fathers would have thought impossible.

But this second post-war era was different—now the peace was uneasy, so that it became "the cold war". And

so this time there was no slacking off : aircraft development
went ahead everywhere with near-emergency speed and
priority. And now the new machines were designed to
carry nuclear weapons—the explosive and destructive
power of a single bomb exceeded that of all the high explosive expended *by both sides* in the recent global conflict.

The world had resolved into just two camps—East and
West—and it was no longer the politicians who held
the power of life or death. It was the scientists, the technic-
ians, the engineers. The runners in the technological
race.

On both sides of the Iron Curtain, some were devoted
to military thinking, some to peaceful thinking ; but each
side strove to keep ahead of the other—to hold the threat
of runaway supremacy. The world's fate literally hung—
still hangs—on the imaginations and skills of a faceless,
largely anonymous, science-army.

And imagination and skill there were in plenty. Britain's
Frank Whittle had first opened up vast new horizons by
inventing his jet engine, with its incredible thrust and
lightness—and everywhere the researchers and designers
were sparked off as seldom before. Strange shapes began
to appear daily in the skies all over the world ; undreamed-
of speeds were reached almost as a matter of routine ;
manned rockets to the Moon and beyond suddenly leapt
off the pages of science fiction on to the drawing boards of
reality.

At first, though, the general public knew little of this
immense activity going on in the security-walled laboratories and drawing offices. Secrecy was part of the race.
Only when the theories had been worked out and checked
mathematically, when the scale models had been built and
tested in wind tunnels, did the startling, weird-shaped

prototypes begin to nose out of the locked hangars, to be put to the final and only real test—in the air.

And for each prototype, there had to be a pilot. Part-flyer, part-technician—and all the way a pioneer, ready to gamble his life in entering the Unknown.

Christmas Eve, 1952. The early morning sky over southern England was heavy with snow clouds and a cold, gusty wind swirled the dead leaves in restless, rustling whirlpools. In patches the sky was mild blue. " Outlook uncertain," said the forecast. Hazelden felt cheated. He would have to go to the airfield after all—possibly only to hang about for hours on the chance that conditions would improve.

At breakfast he broke the news to his wife and their young daughter, Valerie. " Just a little job I really ought to clear up," he told them. " I'll be back for supper."

As he drove out to Boscombe Down airfield, he wondered if his wife, Esma, had realised the truth—that if the clouds *did* clear, and the wind fell a little, he would make the first test-flight of Britain's newest, mightiest and most revolutionary bomber : the four-jet Handley Page Victor.

Hazleden—tall, very broadly built, with springy brown hair—had been a Handley Page test pilot for five years now. As an R.A.F. bomber captain during the war he had gained two D.F.C.s and a reputation for icy calmness in hot situations ; to his crew this big, broad man, sitting up there in front of the bellowing bomber, always seemed solid, secure. Unshakable.

The war flying record he finished up with was impressive —and just as well, for it was all he had, apart from a little money. It would have been stupid to throw away all his experience, not to use his great natural talent as a peace-time pilot.

Handley Page, Britain's oldest aircraft manufacturing concern, had turned out some of the most successful planes of two wars, and had pioneered the country's civil services. Now, with the jet age rapidly emerging, the firm's founder, Sir Frederick Handley Page, was urging his designers to tackle the myriad problems of the day with boldness and imagination. He was convinced that British brains, craftsmanship and courage could by-pass the many stages of intermediate development and experimental flying contemplated by the United States and other countries and, in one leap, reach the era of the jet-bomber ahead of the world. It was, of course, a tremendous gamble—but the whole history of British air power was the story of calculated risks.

The firm's chief designer was Reginald Stafford, F.R.Ae.S. —lanky, bespectacled, with grey-flecked temples and a boyish, quick-smiling face. Immediately after the Nazi surrender, " Staff " had toured German aircraft factories and had been intrigued by the unconventional wing-shape of a new Arado jet-fighter.

In the last year of the war both Allied and German designers had started to think in terms of swept-back and " delta " wings, to achieve extra speed for the new jet-powered fighters. But pronounced sweepback produced serious problems, including poor control qualities at low speeds, on approach and on landing, and treacherous stalling characteristics.

The Arado's wing was swept back, but with a difference : the leading edge curved smoothly, so that the sweepback was progressively decreased from root to tip. " Staff " saw in this a startling possibility—a chance of combining the advantages of both the "delta" shape and the old-fashioned "straight", or rectangular, wing. He made some rapid, rough sketches on the back of an envelope...

Back home, he began work immediately at his drawing board. By the time Hazelden joined the firm a few months later a large, well-organised research group was busy on "Project H.P.-80," striving to produce a four-jet heavy bomber with a revolutionary "crescent" wing.

To Hazelden the drawings of the new machine seemed at first like something out of a science fiction magazine—she was more like a spaceship than an aeroplane. But "Staff" and his "boffins" were being wholly realistic. They were working in strict accordance with Air Ministry specifications for V-bombers. And if their theories proved correct, Britain would gain an aircraft with at least two-and-a-half times the performance of the most successful war-time "heavies".

Handley Page christened their unborn brainchild the "Victor". She would carry no machine-guns—her only defence would be her superior performance. She would cruise very close to the speed of sound, and therefore enemy interceptors would be forced either to endure the severe buffeting of the sound barrier—which would make accurate aiming and shooting next to impossible—or to break through to supersonic speed, in which case they must flash past their quarry at considerably greater velocity and have only a second or so in which to line up their sights and fire.

Inevitably in such a bold, new concept there were many hold-ups and heartbreaks. And tragedy too, when in August 1951 a small-scale model broke up in mid-air and crashed. The pilot, Flight Lieutenant Dougie Broomfield, D.F.M., one of the Handley Page test team, was killed.

(Normally Hazelden would have been flying the scale model, but at sixteen stone and six-foot-one he was much too big for the cockpit).

Anxiously, the cause of the break-up was investigated. It wasn't the new wing that had let them down—the fuselage had had an excessive load. There was no time to build another scaled-down version—the full-sized prototype was already under construction. It was this prototype that "Hazel" took out for a taxi-ing test early in December 1952—and which, after three weeks, he asked permission to fly.

And now—driving to Boscombe Down this Christmas Eve—he saw the sky brighten, felt the gusty wind fall away. He knew in his heart the big day had come; knew, too, that with the loss of the small-scale version he would have to take her off the ground with much less knowledge than he would have wanted of actual handling characteristics . . .

On board with him as the gleaming V-bomber rolled down the runway on her ten wheels was the firm's chief observer, Ian Bennett. They had first flown together ten years before, testing war-planes for the Ministry of Supply, and were close friends.

As the giant plane smoothly gathered speed, Hazelden could feel her mounting strength in his big hands, and suddenly was filled with confidence. In a few seconds now he would ease back the stick and bring her off. Then he would have just five or six seconds in which to decide whether to go on, or to put her down again—to make up his mind whether he was in control of a stable, airworthy craft or "trying to fly a brick."

Still and silent stood the watchers—on the tarmac, in the control tower. The Victor had used only a third of the runway when a thin ribbon of daylight appeared under the wheels. She was airborne and flying steadily, Hazelden holding her a few inches above the concrete. Then his voice came ringing over the radio : " She's a beauty ! " And the pointed nose came up and in a steep, amazingly fast climb the new-born V-bomber entered the boundless element for which she had been designed.

In the months that followed Hazelden flew her at every opportunity. In each aspect of performance tested, the Victor exceeded her design features. Details were secret, but estimates based on statements from " high places " credited her with a top speed of well over 700 m.p.h., a range of at least 8,000 miles and a ceiling of around 55,000 feet.

But the testing was not over yet. Nor were the tragedies.

On the morning of 14th July, 1953, Hazelden was climbing into the aircraft to carry out tests when he was called away to confer with a visiting expert. Reluctantly he handed over to Flight Lieutenant Ronald Ecclestone, a Welshman of about 30.

Later that afternoon, Hazelden—now in Reading—was met by a grey-faced flying-control officer.

"The Victor's crashed—a complete write-off ! "

Flying low over Cranfield airfield in Bedfordshire, the tail unit had come off. She'd dived straight into the ground from about 150 feet. Ecclestone and the three observers on board—Bruce Heithersay, Albert Cook and Hazelden's old friend Ian Bennett—had died instantly.

The cause was diagnosed as a purely local failure, very probably due to metal fatigue in a few of the bolts which held the high-set tailplane in position on the fin. The cure was obvious, simple and certain—and Victor Two was ready for the 1954 Farnborough display.

Now, at last, the British public and the Allied experts watched the softly hissing giant flash low over the airfield, banking first one way and then the other to show off her crescent-shaped wings. The world was convinced that she was sound and reliable, yet another important success for the British aircraft industry.

And much of the credit rightly went to the big, broad, ice-calm man with the sure and sensitive hands who, on that Christmas Eve with the " uncertain outlook," had pioneered a new concept in jet flight—with highest courage had flown the test and proved that the designers' startling new theories were wholly, gloriously practical.

It is one thing to boldly design aircraft to fly faster, probe higher into the outskirts of unknown Space; and another thing to fly them. . . . In the field of fighter development, for instance, many strange and vicious enemies were being encountered—pilots suffered from high altitude bends, impairment of vision, gas pains, dehydration. There was the problem of baling-out, too—what would happen to an airman who had to abandon his jet at anything from five hundred to one thousand m.p.h., perhaps in thin and icy atmosphere ?

In the United States a whole new science was rapidly growing to answer such problems—aero-medicine. Its practitioners were not white-coated test tube watchers : they were practical men, men of impressive courage and dedication who believed in experiencing the problems for themselves—acting as their own guinea pigs. Men like Lieutenant-Colonel John Paul Stapp, U.S. Air Force.

Eldest of four sons of an American Baptist missionary, Stapp was brought up in Bahia, Brazil. Frail, skinny and shy, for a long time he was afraid of motor cars.

A fatal burning accident to his two-year-old cousin shocked him deeply. At the time he was studying English at Baylor University, Texas. He decided to give it up and become a doctor.

Family funds were low, and he took part-time work—washing cars, serving in bars and cafés—to pay his way through medical school. It was not until 1943 that he at last graduated. A year later, Dr. Stapp became Lieut. Stapp, U.S. Medical Corps.

Soon after the war he was posted to the Aero-Medical Laboratory of the Air Command, Dayton, Ohio. And here he found his true vocation—his passionate obsession, the new and strange field of research which was to take command of his life.

He threw himself into the researches with an enthusiasm amounting almost to fanaticism, and spent more time in the air in those early months than in the labs. He field-tested and improved a new emergency breathing device, developed a number of valuable preventive measures for bends and dehydration. Quickly he became a legend to modern jet-pilots. They declared that Stapp knew more about flying " than many of us who have spent our adult lives in the cockpit."

Meanwhile, in other areas of America, rapid progress was being made on other projects—the attack on Space itself. Dominating this drive to reach the stars was a burly, brilliant young German who a few years previously had been forced to stand by and watch Hitler turn his early space-probe rockets into devastating weapons of war. In 1944 many a gaping, jagged crater all over London testified to the arrival of the V.2., and the rocket age.

The young German was Wernher von Braun. As the Reich reeled under the force of the final Allied attacks,

he had been ordered to destroy his equipment. He refused
and, with most of his research team, loaded trucks with
key parts and blueprints, and drove deep into Bavaria. The
Gestapo hunted them, with orders to kill. But when
Allied troops advanced to within range von Braun sent
a message from his mountain hide-out—inviting them to
come and accept the surrender of the world's most experienced rocket experts.

So it was that this outstanding young scientist from the
former enemy country became boss of the vast U.S.
development programme of rocketry for both military
and Space-probe uses. There were other scientists who
doubted whether Man could withstand the "hostile
stresses" of Space. Von Braun—who applied for, and
was granted, U.S. citizenship—answered the doubters.

"Everything in Space obeys the laws of physics,"
he said. "If you know these laws, and obey them, Space
will treat you kindly."

Still many distinguished engineers and medical men
remained unconvinced. The human body could never
bear the physical strains. "Man's inventive power has
outrun the physical powers of his body," they said.
"We may send machines into Space, but they will be
unmanned."

Stapp's reaction to these pessimistic predictions was
quick and typical. He shared von Braun's confidence and
determination.

"Why are we always underrating the human body?"
he demanded. And he cited the way athletics records
were being improved year after year.

"The only limits are *psychological*—man goes on improving his physical capabilities all the time."

And now Stapp made a momentous decision—he would

stake his own life to prove that mortal man was not nearly so vulnerable as von Braun's critics believed.

He plunged himself with all his customary enthusiasm into the newest and strangest branch of medicine, bio-astronautics. His chief concern was with " G "—the sudden large increase in gravitational " pull ", causing temporary loss of vision and mental black-out, that fighter pilots had already encountered, and which the new Spacemen would be encountering many times more severely as they were blasted off, strapped in tiny capsules atop their ultra-high-acceleration rockets.

Stapp designed for his experiments a rocket-propelled " sled," running on rails, capable of very high speeds. Towards the end of its 2,600 feet of track, the rails ran across a pool of water reaching almost up to the level of the sled's runners. Into this pool the sled's water brakes —large, metal scoops projecting down under its belly— would plough, jolting it to a stop *in a matter of one-to-two seconds*.

The first passenger was a thirteen-stone dummy, christened by the team "Oscar Eightball". At first all went well, but when the rocket thrust was increased and the sled travelled faster the jolt of the brakes biting into the water made Oscar break his harness, smash through a windbreak of one-inch pine and soar into the air to land 700 feet away.

The team was awed, dismayed, as they picked up the mangled remains of the dummy. But not Stapp.

" Well, looks like we need a stronger harness, boys," he said.

On 10th December, 1947, he took the first ride himself— a single-rocket spurt that reached only about 100 m.p.h. Next day three rockets were fired, and the sled did 200 m.p.h. Because of the need to determine the effects on different types of physique and various age groups, others took the hair-raising ride, too—but Stapp never asked them to do anything he had not tried personally.

The programme reached its climax when the sled, with Stapp as the passenger, reached 632 m.p.h.—faster than a .45 calibre bullet. It stopped dead in just 1.4 seconds, and he experienced 40 G's—roughly *six times greater than a Spaceman must undergo during a rocket take off.* In that brief 1.4 seconds, his normal weight of twelve stone was increased to 480 stone; the jolt was equivalent to that which a car driver would experience hitting a brick wall at 50 m.p.h. Yet Stapp suffered no permanent injury.

During these experiments, many of his friends pleaded with him to stop. His doctor-brother Celso warned him : " You pull out of each ride successfully, but who can tell what the cumulative damage to your system may be ? "

Yet Stapp's faith in the toughness of the human frame was as firm as ever. He knew the risks—for one thing, no one could be certain that the sudden, violent impact of the braking would not detach the retinas of his eyes and cause permanent blindness—but he went on. And then a new, stronger sled was built, and Stapp announced his intention to take a ride on it at 1,000 m.p.h.

The importance of his experiments, and his contribution to the success of the Space programme and the safety of the astronauts, has been widely recognised. His many decorations include the Legion of Merit with Oak Leaf Cluster, and the U.S. Air Force's Cheney Award for valour and self-sacrifice. But perhaps his greatest, most warming reward comes from the men he serves—the jet-pilots and astronauts. They have gone on record with the flat statement that he is doing more for the flyers of the future than all the backroom, "armchair" research being conducted in laboratories and rocket bases throughout the U.S.A.

John Paul Stapp—who was once afraid of motor cars—has become the "fastest man on Earth." And working principally on the ground, has won a place in history as a hero of the sky.

Crescent wings . . . aircraft flying higher, faster, more safely with every year that passes . . . manned capsules orbiting the world, rockets trail-blazing into deep Space. In sixty years, aviation has journeyed from Kitty Hawk to Venus. For the future, the sky is no longer the limit.

Other planets beckon.

But to build the future, you have to ensure the present. The Western nations believe the best way to prevent another war is to build up nuclear strength and efficiency. To this end, rockets of incredible complexity and devastating destructive power have been evolved—standing ready to retaliate, within seconds, against any aggressor.

Yet the modern missile, marvel though it is, cannot foresee *all* the dangers and counter-measures opposing its path to its target—or if it does " see " them, it probably will fail to understand them. In other words, the missile's electronic brain can never entirely replace the mind of a highly-trained human pilot. Nor can a missile report after its mission "target destroyed," or "near miss". And since the main reason for its existence is to prevent a global war, another disadvantage is that it cannot be used in limited operations—" small wars," rebellions or local conflicts.

Missiles cannot search for armoured columns on the move, nor strafe goods trains. They cannot carry infantry

or paratroops; they cannot fly commanders and staff
officers from battle area to battle area, and they cannot
take aerial photographs of enemy positions and bring them
back to base. Obviously, in anything short of a large-
scale, all-out nuclear conflict, all these jobs would have to
be done—and done efficiently. And so for a long time
to come, manned aircraft will still have a vital role in
defence.

The American government recognises this as well as
anyone—while pouring billions of dollars into missile
development, it still maintains the strongest air armada the
world has known : the U.S. Strategic Air Command.

Patrolling the free world in giant B-52 eight-jet machines,
America's most skilled and experienced pilots are eternally
vigilant. With bases strung all around the globe, S.A.C.
to-day is undoubtedly an equally decisive factor for the
preservation of peace as the West's mounting stock of
long-range missiles.

B-52's have flown non-stop around the world in just
44 hours. The plane's huge, swept-back wings are flexible
—they literally flap up and down like a bird's in flight,
through an arc of 28 feet ! Among its hundreds of secret
devices is the uncanny radar bombsight which, having been
fed the right information, makes all the necessary compen-
sations itself with its 110,000 separate parts. The bombs
could be dropped from nine miles up, through the foulest
weather, with pinpoint accuracy.

The crews have to be tough as well as skilful, for the
job of flying these giants is cruel labour, mentally and
physically. On an average flight, even before they get off
the ground the crews have three hours of briefing—a
vital process of planning and calculation which demands
utmost concentration and meticulous checking. And the

pilots' pre-take-off check list runs to more than twenty pages. . . .

The average flight lasts ten hours. Many of the men suffer severe muscular fatigue caused by prolonged sitting in cramped positions with the vibration of the eight jets hammering through the seats. Duodenal ulcers—the result of tension—are not uncommon.

Few of the B-52 flyers are young : pilots must have more than 1,500 hours of flying before they are even considered for this elite force. Navigators have to be trained in the operation of dozens of new, complicated, top-secret gadgets so that they become experts in electronics and radar as well. So, S.A.C. is full of beribboned veterans—thorough, prudent, steady men, who take a deep pride in their immense responsibility.

The Command's huge force—they're also equipped with some B-47's, almost the equal of the B-52s—is on the alert twenty-four hours a day, every day of the year. The entire armada, from its multitude of bases, could be in the air and on the way to its targets, fully armed, within twenty minutes. So enormous is its striking power that only the President of the United States can order it to drop nuclear bombs on an enemy. But it can also be employed in limited operations—using weapons of various size and power, tailor-made for different types of target.

Patrols and training flights are almost constantly in the air. Every S.A.C. man is ready, but he hopes he never will be ordered to drop his nuclear bomb. His job, as he sees it, is firstly to be strong and efficient—to make it clear that war cannot pay, that any major attack on the free nations will be punished by instant, sure and utter ruin. Secondly, in local conflicts to try and restore order and prevent the trouble spreading by a show of invincible strength—and if that fails, to carry out strikes with small-size bombs on key military targets.

These super-armed, highly-skilled and experienced aviators constitute the free world's most powerful weapon —a huge and highly complex organisation of men and machines which, in just over fifty years, has evolved out of the flimsy, tottering contraptions of the Wrights, Santos-Dumont, Blériot and Farman. Into the stratosphere, girdling the globe, they carry the pride and courage of their calling—the same spirit that burned in Albert Ball, Billy Bishop, Billy Mitchell, Wiley Post, Amy Johnson, Cobber Kain, John Cruickshank, Lydia Litviak, Geoffrey de Havilland, John Derry and all the others who have gone before.

But now that spirit is tempered with a sense of awesome responsibility ; for theirs is a task no airmen ever before have faced. A task which, even in time of peace, even though their names are unknown to most of us, gives everyone of them a place among the heroes of the sky.

Potentially, they are the greatest destroyers ever to appear on this planet, but they use their strength and authority only to police the skies. And they like to call themselves " the planet's peace patrol ".